# Praise for A Military Guide To Property Investing

'To quote a phrase from this book, "Bravo Zulu" to Lachlan and Tori for writing such an impressive and unique guide to strategic property investment. Their respective military backgrounds have enabled them to craft 10 easy-to-implement steps that create a targeted pathway to property investment success.'

Nicola McDougall
Former Editor, *Australian Property Investor* magazine, and Co-founder, Bricks & Mortar Media

'It was a pleasure to read a property investment hard copy with raw substance about Lachlan and Tori's pathway to property success and strategies that can be initiated to find your own pathway to property investment success.

'With military precision, discipline and systematic vision of your goals and objectives, you too can have a strong portfolio.

'I am excited to see the adventure Lachlan and Tori are about to go on in the near future. They have created such a strong platform and business on the back of hard work and their passion for property. A five-star read for anyone about to go on their own property journey!'

Jeremy Iannuzzelli
Partner, Keshab Chartered Accountants

# A Military Guide To

# PROPERTY INVESTING

## A TARGETED APPROACH TO CONQUERING YOUR GOALS

**LACHLAN VIDLER**
**TORI COLLS**

*To Merissa, Brian, Rebecca and all our*
*friends and family who have supported us on our journey,*
**Thank you for believing in our vision.**

First published in 2021 by Major Street Publishing Pty Ltd
PO Box 106, Highett, Vic. 3190
E: info@majorstreet.com.au  W: majorstreet.com.au  M: +61 421 707 983

NATIONAL
LIBRARY
OF AUSTRALIA

A catalogue record for this book is available
from the National Library of Australia

Printed book: 978-1-922611-06-2
Ebook: 978-1-922611-07-9

Cover design by Tess McCabe
Internal design by Production Works
Printed in Australia by Ovato, an Accredited ISO AS/NZS 14001:2004
Environmental Management System Printer.

10 9 8 7 6 5 4 3 2 1

# CONTENTS

# Preface

# YOUR PATHWAY TO PROPERTY

It feels like a lifetime ago that we commenced our military and property-investing journeys. Over the years, we've gained a wealth of knowledge and skills from our time spent within the Australian Defence Force (ADF) and the business world. As many serving and ex-serving members would know, your experiences within the military inevitably shape your perspective forever. Military members see, think, feel and interpret life through a completely different lens than those who haven't served, and we strongly believe that this provides us with a powerful perspective on investing and goal achievement. The military taught us lifelong skills that we feel privileged to apply to every aspect of our lives, including our tertiary education, investment portfolio, personal and professional relationships, and our dealings in our own business and the wider industry. Now, we want to share those skills and perspectives with other avid and like-minded investors.

Since commencing our own unique military journeys, we've had the privilege of combining our portfolios, business acumen and military knowledge to create a thriving buyer's agency business and investment portfolio. Our personal portfolio includes a range of residential investment properties, domestic and international share-holdings, and investments in several luxury property developments. Founding, developing and scaling our business and portfolio hasn't come easily. Like all investments, it was built upon a foundation of sleepless nights, years of learning, relationship growth, revelations and failures. But through perseverance, adaptability and unwavering determination, we were able to formulate a portfolio that works for us – and this book will teach you those fundamental lessons so that you can do the same.

## LACHLAN'S PROPERTY PATHWAY

Growing up, I moved around a lot with my family. My father was a business executive, and this meant that we needed to move to wherever his next job would take us. By the time I was 10 years old, I had lived in Sydney, Brisbane, Melbourne and Auckland – sometimes multiple times in each city! Looking back, I can see how much the moving was beneficial to my development as a young person.

We eventually came back and settled in Sydney for my time in high school. When the global financial crisis (GFC) hit, my father was one of the unlucky casualties and he lost his job. Unfortunately, he struggled to find work after this, and that meant that my mother had to support me, my father and my sister throughout my time in high school. For me, this was a pivotal moment in my own journey. I had seen my family go from being wealthy and fortunate to suddenly being thrown into financial uncertainty.

As I got older, I knew that I wanted to join the military. I saw that it would give me the opportunity to get out of home, learn fantastic skills and travel the world for a job. I was far from a perfect student for most of my school years – I got a 30 out of 100 for my final mathematics mark in Year 10. I certainly didn't hate school, but I was quite a lazy student and I expected that I'd just magically start getting better marks without putting in any of the hard work.

This all changed when I realised that I wouldn't be able to join the Navy if I didn't pick my marks up. So, from late in Year 11 until

I graduated, I invested any time that I wasn't playing sport or socialising with friends into studying and trying to improve my academics. Through a lot of hard work – that certainly would've been easier if I'd just applied myself throughout all of high school and not just the last 12 months – I did well enough in my Higher School Certificate to gain entry to the Navy and university.

## My military and civilian career

I joined the Royal Australian Navy at age 18 and immediately went to HMAS *Creswell* where Navy officers complete their initial training. It was an incredible experience being able to move out of home at such a young age and start a job that brought new and exciting experiences every single day.

After finishing my training at HMAS *Creswell*, I moved back to Sydney and was posted to HMAS *Watson* to begin my Maritime Warfare Officer training, and then to HMAS *Choules* for my first sea posting. Maritime Warfare Officers are tasked with the navigation of the vessel and are responsible for the safety of the ship at sea. During my time on HMAS *Choules*, I was fortunate to be deployed on my first military operation – Operation Render Safe. Operation Render Safe sees allied nations like Australia, New Zealand, the United Kingdom and the United States remove old World War II explosives from various islands in the South Pacific. My experience took me to Bougainville, Papua New Guinea, and it was incredible to see the positive impact we had on local villages by making their homes safer for them.

I then spent three years at the Australian Defence Force Academy (ADFA) in Canberra, where I completed university studies as well as further training. Although I had finished the first stages of my tertiary education, I knew that I wanted to learn more. So, I enrolled in a Master of Commerce (Finance) through the University of New South Wales (UNSW).

After graduating from ADFA, I moved back to Sydney to continue further training. My next sea posting would see me sent north to Darwin, where our fleet of patrol boats is based. During my time in Darwin, I was posted to HMAS *Bathurst* and deployed on my second military operation – Operation Resolute. Operation Resolute sees ships patrol our northern waters to enforce customs, fisheries and immigration law. After my time in Darwin, I moved back to Sydney, and I decided to make a career change from Maritime Warfare Officer to Maritime Logistics Officer. I always knew that the Navy was not going to be my forever job and a move into logistics would set me up for a business career after my time in the Navy; there are not many ships to navigate when you become a civilian!

After completing logistics officer training at HMAS *Cerberus* on Victoria's Mornington Peninsula, I moved back to – you guessed it – Sydney. I was happily posted to HMAS *Success*, where I was a member of her decommissioning crew after she spent 33 years in service. My final sea deployment saw me conduct a regional engagement activity known as Indo-Pacific Endeavour. This involved sailing throughout South-East Asia to countries such as Malaysia, Singapore and Indonesia, and conducting missions with our partners in the region to enhance relationships with our neighbours.

My final posting was to HMAS *Waterhen*, which is a base in the north of Sydney where I helped deliver logistical support to a fleet of smaller naval vessels. During this posting, I decided that it was time for a new challenge and that I was ready to discharge from the Navy to begin my business career.

After leaving the Navy, I moved directly into management consulting with Deloitte. Management consulting is best described as being brought in by companies and government departments to help them identify problems and provide them with the tools and solutions to fix their issues. I was extremely fortunate to work for two global powerhouses in the consulting world: Deloitte and Accenture.

With the skills and expertise I learned from my time in the Navy and consolidated in the business and consulting world, I commenced my new career as a buyer's agent and founded Atlas Property Group.

## My first property purchase

I wish that I could say I was a diligent investor from the beginning, saving every penny and making great financial decisions. I made many of the same silly decisions that most young people make: ridiculous cars, holidays, eating out and other less-than-ideal uses of my money. Fortunately, I kicked this approach and began to save money and educate myself, which led me to my first property purchase at the age of 22.

My first property was a solid brick, three-bedroom house in the Brisbane area purchased for $260,000 and rented out for $330 per week. Although I look back and can now see that there were better purchases out there, this property has been a solid performer that still fits neatly into our overall property portfolio. The property is now worth over $310,000 and has grown at an annualised rate of around 6 per cent – not a bad result for a first property.

## What motivates me

I have always loved the idea of investing and creating a better financial future for myself and my family. I remember being a teenager and trying to learn about investing so that I could build the best life for myself that I could. As I have gotten older, I'm still motivated by a desire to improve my own life, but I also want to help other people do the same.

As I have learned through my formal education as well as through life experiences, knowledge is power. If somebody doesn't understand what or how to invest, how could they possibly do it? This thought motivates me to want to help people create better financial futures for themselves through utilising the power of property.

Everyday Australians have opportunities to invest in property, but so many people genuinely struggle to make sound investments. By taking the knowledge that we give our clients and have now written into this book, more people will be able to set themselves up for better and more comfortable retirements.

## TORI'S PROPERTY PATHWAY

From as early as I can remember, I knew business and investing was the path I would eventually take in my career. But first, I wanted to travel, study and let adventure find me. That's why joining the Royal Australian Air Force (RAAF) was such an easy decision. When I decided to join the ADF, I was excited and determined to walk out of the local recruiting office with an offer for an Aircrew Officer role. After many months, I walked out with something incredibly different – a job offer to become an Intelligence Officer through ADFA in Canberra.

My family and I were elated that I was going to train to become an officer in the RAAF, and no-one was prouder than Mum and Dad. Growing up, my parents taught me the importance of working hard, setting goals and continuous learning. Together, they taught me everything I know about saving money, investing whenever and wherever I can, living within my means and setting financial milestones.

When I was 13, our lives were changed forever when Mum was diagnosed with motor neurone disease – a debilitating, terminal illness with no known cure. These years were the hardest for Mum and my family to overcome, but thanks to the help of our incredible friends and family, we were able to provide Mum with the highest quality of care at home.

Five years later, when I was in my first year of the military, Mum passed away. We were all rocked with grief and I don't think any of us were prepared for the gaping hole that would be left in our hearts. But through Mum's struggles, she taught us all the art of resilience, strength and fierce independence, which she had embodied for so many years. I couldn't be prouder of her and my family, and I thank them every day for supporting me through the good and the difficult times.

Thanks to the valuable life lessons that Mum imparted, I was able to walk into my latter university years and military career with an informed and focused mindset – and I certainly wouldn't have the portfolio that I have today without Mum and Dad's sage advice. These lessons have been captured throughout the pages of this book and enabled me to make my first purchase during my first year of tertiary studies (more on that first property later).

**My military career**

After receiving my commission as an officer and my first tertiary degree, I undertook Intelligence Officer training in the RAAF. During one of my first jobs as a qualified officer, I was posted to one of Australia's strategic intelligence agencies, the Defence Intelligence Organisation (DIO). Strategic intelligence agencies are tasked with the important duty of producing timely assessments on international issues, based on a range of intelligence sources. These assessments are given directly to senior Defence leadership and government ministers so that they are aware of all international events as they occur. These briefs form the basis of high-level decision-making by our government.

During my time at DIO, I learned important skills such as time-critical analysis, military strategy and strategic thinking. My job was to utilise these skills across a wide range of analytical areas, from geopolitics to advanced weaponry, which I found incredibly interesting as a young officer. I was excited to go to work every day, and I knew that the work my team and I were doing was critical to protecting Australia's national interests. I felt like I was finally working towards something that was greater than myself.

During my time spent in strategic and operational postings, I was fortunate to achieve my goal of domestic and international travel. I lived in multiple capital cities across Australia and worked alongside incredible people at a range of military units. I was privileged to go on multiple trips to train and work at the Defense Intelligence Agency in Washington, DC, and liaise with like-minded colleagues at the Pentagon. During these visits, it was incredibly rewarding to work alongside Australia's allies on the other side of the globe as we worked towards achieving the same mission. These were critical and defining moments in my life, and they showed me that hard work and chasing opportunities can and will take you anywhere.

At the same time as travelling, training and working, I knew I wanted to keep learning and developing myself as an officer and as a businesswoman. I chose to continue my own personal development by completing my Master of Project Management. I knew this degree would assist me when I decided to transition from the RAAF into a business-based career, and I also knew that it would help me advance my personal property portfolio, particularly for property development.

### My first property purchase

I knew I wanted to implement the advice I'd gained growing up and begin building my own personal property portfolio as soon as possible. Rather than spend my wage on holidays or material items, I started to follow a savings plan that was dedicated to purchasing my first property. Like the majority of first-time buyers, I wanted to buy in an area that I knew well, which was home in Albury, New South Wales. Luckily for me, I also have an incredible Dad who was able to guide me with his experience and advice throughout the buying process.

My first purchase was a quaint two-bedroom unit in a quiet, residential estate, purchased for $210,000. The property is now valued at $300,000 at an annualised growth rate of 7.39 per cent – not a bad start out of the gate! Even today, this property still fits into our personal portfolio strategy – our aim is to hold established, positive-cash-flow properties that generate above-average market growth. My first property taught me a myriad of lessons that I've been able to take forward in my investing journey, and I'm elated to have the opportunity to share these with you.

### What motivates me

Financial investment, property development and business captured my interest from a very young age. After growing up learning valuable investment basics, I knew I wanted to share my knowledge with other young people who also wanted to strive for their own version of financial freedom and independence. Let's face it, personal finance can be a conversation killer at any party. But the more I spoke to family, friends, colleagues and clients about what was working for me in my personal portfolio, the more I realised that investing is a topic on everyone else's minds, too.

Although I knew the military was always going to be a stepping stone for me in my career, it taught me lifelong lessons. I learned the value of remaining disciplined, dedicated, courageous and loyal to my own self-improvement and investment journey. These values helped me make the life-changing decision to commit my career to helping others achieve financial freedom through embodying the habits and values that I learned during my time in the RAAF.

Since the barrier to entry with property is higher than other investments, property can seem like a daunting investment for a young person to dive into. I want to break down those barriers for anyone who's determined to enter the market or looking to strengthen their existing portfolio. Generally, property is an excellent, stable and sustainable investment strategy – if the fundamentals are implemented. Any investment takes courage, and showing other people that they're capable of taking control of their financial future is what drives me. I'm excited and honoured to have the opportunity to share the lessons I've learned with you.

## OUR JOURNEY TOGETHER

As young investors, we both knew that we wanted to dedicate our careers to making property investing more accessible to Australians from all walks of life, while passing on the valuable skills that we both learned throughout our military careers. We have always had a strong passion for finding excellent investment-grade properties so we could continue to bolster our own thriving portfolios, and we knew we wanted to help others do the same.

From this idea, Atlas Property Group was formed. Atlas Property Group is an exclusive buyer's agency that connects investors with high-quality, well-researched investment properties in high-performing markets. We advocate on our clients' behalf and source them investment-grade properties that we know will help them achieve their personal investment goals and set them on their path to financial freedom.

We've remained dedicated to our personal mission to deliver an unbeatable service to our client base through our personal commitment to tertiary education. To achieve this, we are both studying our third tertiary degree (each): a Master of Property Investment and Development.

Our investment journey has enabled us to live life on our own terms while helping everyday Australians along the way. We have created a business and a lifestyle that enables us to be our own bosses, coupled with an investment portfolio that produces a passive income that helps us achieve our own version of financial freedom. We hope that after reading this book, you're able to take away some of the valuable lessons that we've learned on your own investing journey.

It's time to take control of your financial future. Your time is now. Let's begin.

*Lachlan and Tori*

### Lachlan Vidler
**Director and Founder, Atlas Property Group**

Master of Commerce (Finance), University of New South Wales
Master of Property Investment and Development (undertaking),
  Western Sydney University
Graduate Certificate of Property Investment, Western Sydney University
Bachelor of Business, University of New South Wales

Member of Property Investment Professionals of Australia
Member of Property Investors Council of Australia
Buyer's Agent – Licensed Agent (multiple states and territories)

### Tori Colls
**General Manager, Atlas Property Group**

Master of Project Management, University of New South Wales
Master of Property Investment and Development (undertaking),
  Western Sydney University
Bachelor of Business, University of New South Wales

Officer of the RAAF
Member of Australian Institute of Project Management
Member of Property Investment Professionals of Australia
Buyer's Agent – Licensed Agent

# Step 1:
# REVEILLE

Originally a drum beat, reveille has been played on bugles, trumpets, pipes and drums to wake sleeping soldiers and prepare them for the day ahead. Stemming from the French word *réveillez*, meaning 'wake up', reveille has continued in contemporary use at military ceremonies, funerals and in barracks around the country.

This book is your reveille.

**Step 1: Reveille**

Step 2: Discipline

Step 3: Teamwork

Step 4: Professional mastery

Step 5: Excellence

Step 6: Mission analysis

Step 7: Courage

Step 8: Adaptability and flexibility

Step 9: Dedication

Step 10: Loyalty

## Step 1: Reveille

While the sleeping soldier heard the tune dance across the battle-field, you are reading your own battle tune as you prepare to awaken into your first days as a property investor. Your stakes may be different to those that soldiers face, but your reveille is just as important in the context of your financial future. Whether you are in your 20s or your 50s, there is always something that can be done to provide you with a more comfortable and secure financial future. While your strategies and approach may change based on factors such as age and income, you must listen to your own reveille to wake up and begin your journey.

We wish we could sit here and tell you that your journey will be easy, that you will experience daily success, that your friends and family will look at you green with envy from the moment you finish this book. Unfortunately, your journey will not be as easy, calm or straightforward as this. We are so excited to share with you all the tools for success in property investing, but it will not be without hard work, dedication and courage on your part. As the saying goes, 'You can lead a horse to water, but you can't make it drink.' Although we share all of our secrets, methods and approaches to investing in this book, if you aren't prepared to put in the hard work, then this information probably won't help you on your investing journey.

Thankfully, we have written this book to give you every chance at success! We have broken down the property-investing process into 10 easy-to-implement steps that each focus on the core tenets for success as both a military professional and a property investor. These topics range from teamwork to courage, professional mastery to loyalty and many others. The military is renowned for producing exceptional people and cutting-edge products; that's why you often hear terms like 'military-grade' to denote a particularly high-quality product. We have taken our years of military experience, combined it with our property investing and business knowledge and overlaid our master's-level university education to bring you this guide. By following all of the information in *A Military Guide To Property Investing*, you will be well positioned for property investment success and long-term wealth creation that gives you a strong financial future.

## WHY INVESTING IS IMPORTANT

It's no secret that the Great Australian Dream of owning your own home on a quarter-acre block has become harder to achieve with each passing year. Wages have remained stagnant for most of the past two decades, inflation has trickled along at a snail's pace and we've experienced two recent and significant economic downturns: the GFC and the COVID-19 pandemic. It's no wonder so many Australians are missing out on achieving their property dreams when the market fundamentals that help realise this are no longer present. Whether your dream is that quarter-acre block, more time with family or the financial freedom to have more choice, it is clear that these highly desired goals are harder to achieve than ever before.

While financial freedom is difficult to achieve, it's certainly not impossible! The reason most people fall short of attaining financial freedom is that they continue to trade their time for a salary. Unfortunately, as we've just mentioned, wages have stagnated, forcing people to continually devote more time to working while receiving less benefit (wages) for doing so. The solution to this problem is to invest your money. As you read this book, the reasons why we have chosen property as our vehicle of wealth will become abundantly clear. If you invested $100 each month for the next 35 years, you would have invested $42,000. With a 7 per cent return per annum, which is extremely achievable in property, you would earn almost $140,000 for a total balance of over $180,000. As you can see, for a small monthly investment, a person can dramatically change the course of their financial future. If these are the results from such a small amount, imagine what can be achieved by purchasing only a few properties to set you up for financial freedom!

While we just talked about why investing is important from a money perspective, money is not everything. Money should be thought of as the vehicle rather than the destination. The reason it is important to understand your destination – your end goal – is because it will change how you invest. Some people invest so that they can retire early, whereas others invest so that they can pass something down to future generations. Each of these goals requires a unique approach that will change based upon a number of factors such as timeline, required financial return and risk aversion. Put simply, if you don't understand where you are going, you will never know when you reach your destination.

These are some of the most common reasons that we hear from people on why they want to invest:

- to retire early
- to pass on wealth to future generations
- to create a legacy
- to allow their family to have a higher quality of life
- for financial independence.

There are many reasons why people invest, and these are just some of the most common examples. Ultimately, most people choose to invest because financial freedom reduces their anxiety over their financial position, so they can put this energy into enjoying life with their friends and family.

## OPPORTUNITY COST

One of the most important skills that is taught in the military is the ability to understand the flow-on effects of decisions. On a battle-field, by moving soldiers to one area, you may sacrifice a greater tactical advantage that you could have gained by leaving them where they were originally positioned.

This skill is just as important in your investing journey, where it is commonly referred to as opportunity cost. Opportunity cost is the overall result of making one decision over another. If you choose to buy a new car, you receive the benefit of the new car, but you lose the benefit of holding the money you just spent. The question becomes: was the benefit you received from purchasing the car greater than the loss you feel from spending your money?

I'm sure you've noticed that we keep referring to opportunity cost as a choice. The reason for this is because that is exactly what an opportunity cost is – a choice.

Investing is a choice and there is an opportunity cost to this decision. The benefit of investing is the financial return that you will experience down the track. The tricky decision is whether that future benefit is enough to sacrifice something today, such as a new car or an expensive overseas holiday.

Before you can evaluate the opportunity cost, we think it's important for you to understand exactly what 'opportunity' you are assessing. As medicine continues to increase our life expectancy, the requirement to hold more money at retirement also increases. Today, many people are expected to live for another 25 to 30 years after they retire from the workforce. The advances in medicine, combined with a growing percentage of the population living into their 90s and beyond, is resulting in more older Australians being forced onto the Age Pension due to having insufficient savings.

While the concept of an Age Pension sounds wonderful, the reality is that the current Age Pension is barely above the poverty line. The Association of Superannuation Funds of Australia estimates that people living on the Age Pension can't afford to own a car or hold private health insurance, and can only afford basic clothes and limited leisure activities such as rare trips to the cinema. After a lifetime of working to support a family and build a better life, this does not sound like the retirement any Australian deserves to experience. This scenario is one that we hear too frequently from clients who are hoping to avoid the mistakes of their older family members who are now living in this situation.

When we talk about the opportunity cost of investing, this is the situation that we are talking about. It can be quite a confronting topic for some people, almost like a discussion around their own mortality. It's extremely difficult for anybody to be able to look forward 40-plus years into the future and understand how small sacrifices today will make that future better for themselves and their family. Unfortunately, too many people take an approach of playing hard today and hoping that the future will just magically sort itself out. This is why we advocate making those small changes today, like investing that $100 per month, and watching your financial future gradually become brighter.

We think that the concept of opportunity cost was best summarised by Tom Hanks when he said, 'It's supposed to be hard. If it were easy, everybody would do it.'

## PROPERTY AS A VEHICLE OF WEALTH

By now, we hope that you understand why investing is important for your financial future. With so many opportunities out there, it can be hard to know what the best asset is to invest in so that you can achieve all of your financial goals. For us, the answer is both simple and complicated – property! Before we invested in property, we both invested in shares, bonds and managed funds. These types of investments, particularly shares, are the most common assets that you will hear people talking about when they say that they invest in something. We had successes and failures investing in these different assets before we decided to begin our property-investment journey.

As we slowly watched our different successes and failures unfold, we began to wonder if there was a better approach we could take. We began to investigate other assets and we eventually decided to pursue property after seeing how well it had performed around Australia over the last couple of decades.

For us, deciding on property as our vehicle of wealth became a very simple decision. Almost instantly, we saw how the power of leverage would compound our returns and allow us to receive a greater result than if we continued with our other assets. Leverage – sometimes known as 'other people's money' – is the use of debt to help purchase an asset. In real estate, if you put down a 10 per cent deposit on a $500,000 property you will spend $50,000 and the remaining $450,000 is provided as a home loan from a bank. The power of leverage is that for only $50,000, you are able to acquire an asset that is worth $500,000. The amazing part of leveraging is that you will now achieve capital growth on that $500,000 asset rather than only on the $50,000 you personally contributed.

So that you can see a real-life example of leverage, let's use the example of two of our friends, Joe and Nick. Joe and Nick have both decided that they would like to invest their money so that they can have a more secure financial future. Joe has heard about the power of leverage so he decides that he would like to choose property as his vehicle of wealth. On the other hand, Nick has never heard about leverage and he decides to purchase shares because he thinks it will be easier and will give him a good return.

Joe and Nick each have $50,000 to invest and they both go searching for the best property and shares for them to invest in. Since Joe is purchasing property, he knows that he can use his $50,000 for a 10 per cent deposit and the bank will loan him the remaining money so that he can purchase a $500,000 property. Nick is not able to use leverage in the same way as Joe so he is only able to use his $50,000 to purchase $50,000 in shares. As they both search for their assets to purchase, Joe is able to find a property that he believes will grow in value at an average of 7 per cent each year, while Nick feels very confident that he has purchased shares in a company that will grow at an average of 10 per cent each year. As you can see in table 1.1, even with the higher annual growth of 10 per cent, the overall capital gain of the shares does not even come close to the capital gain of the property. For the same amount of invested money, Joe has been able to turn his $50,000 into a gain of $483,576 whereas Nick has only managed to gain an additional $79,687 – a difference of over $400,000!

Table 1.1: Investing in property versus shares

| Asset | Property | Shares |
|---|---|---|
| Personal contribution | $50,000 | $50,000 |
| Loan value | $450,000 | – |
| Asset value (current) | $500,000 | $50,000 |
| Annual growth | 7% | 10% |
| Asset value (in 10 years) | $983,576 | $129,687 |
| Capital gain | $483,576 | $79,687 |

While leverage was a significant factor in our decision to choose property as our vehicle of wealth, property is overall less risky than shares, and reduced risk greatly appealed to us. Risk is best described as the likelihood that the annual return of the property will deviate from the expected annual return. Most people know this concept as standard deviation. Without boring you with the complicated maths behind it, property is recognised by academics, industry leaders and investment managers as having the highest level of annual returns compared to the risk that you accept by purchasing the property. Overall, with property carrying less risk compared to shares, enjoying higher annual returns for the risk that is accepted and being able to leverage our money into assets that were far greater in value, property was firmly cemented as our chosen vehicle of wealth.

So now you know why we moved towards property as our chosen vehicle of wealth, but what made us stay? Well, first and foremost, we genuinely love property and real estate. Property is something that we are extremely passionate about, and it gives us great joy to help our clients on their own property journeys. For our own financial future, we love that we can add value to our properties to increase our annual growth; that there is very little annual effort required to maintain the portfolio (something we discuss in much greater detail in Step 3 – Teamwork); and there is always a market around Australia that is experiencing growth (the trick is knowing how and where to look!).

We will cover value-adding in Step 5 – Excellence. For now, you just need to know that you can manufacture additional capital growth in your properties by 'adding value'. This value-adding can take many forms, but most often it is through things like small renovations, such as painting or modernising spaces like a kitchen or bathroom. By adding value, you can effectively create additional annual growth that exceeds the cost of the value add. This strategy becomes particularly important when the property cycle reaches a point of capital growth stagnation – you can continue making money when others don't!

In Step 3 – Teamwork, you will find out how important building a team can be. This team is what will allow you to create a property portfolio that requires very little effort to maintain, because you outsource the common tasks to your team members. By having a portfolio that requires limited annual effort from you, you will be able to reap all of the financial benefits of your portfolio without having to regularly break a sweat.

When a new recruit joins the military, they don't wake up on day two of their initial training with a proficient military mindset. It takes a number of days and weeks before a recruit will experience their own reveille and begin adopting the practices of a military professional. Similarly, it takes many years for investors to become comfortable with and capable of dealing in property, which will enable them to achieve financial freedom. *A Military Guide To Property Investing* is here to commemorate your reveille and your personal journey in property. In our experienced opinion, property has proven to be a powerful vehicle of wealth and is a prevailing asset class that investors should focus their attention on. This is the strategy that we have adopted, and we have used it to build a multi-state and multi-region property portfolio that will allow us to be financially free when we choose to retire. We hope that you find this guide a useful and powerful tool to accompany you on your own journey.

# Step 2:
# DISCIPLINE

Discipline lies at the core of all military activities and missions. Soldiers, sailors and airmen and airwomen are often called upon to discharge their duties in some of the harshest conditions and environments on our planet. From hot jungles to cyclones and seas with 30 ft waves, these conditions are not for the fainthearted. Years of practised discipline is what allows ordinary people to continually act in extraordinary ways.

Step 1: Reveille

**Step 2: Discipline**

Step 3: Teamwork

Step 4: Professional mastery

Step 5: Excellence

Step 6: Mission analysis

Step 7: Courage

Step 8: Adaptability and flexibility

Step 9: Dedication

Step 10: Loyalty

## Step 2: Discipline

Investing is hard. There are no two ways about it. Investing is challenging for many reasons, but one of the most significant is that it requires incredible discipline over a long period. For most people, investing begins decades before they will be able to realise the benefits of their investments. We have seen many of our friends, family members and clients run out of steam during their investing journey and give up on their dreams of financial freedom. The discipline ingrained into the military has been captured in stories for centuries – the best investors embody the same characteristics throughout their investing journey. Sacrificing short-term satisfaction for long-term happiness; creating and executing plans and goals; and being willing to learn and improve – these are just some of the traits that come from discipline and are key to success during your investing journey.

In the military, there is a common saying: 'Be brilliant at the basics.' While there are many advanced and complicated methods for doing things, they are all underpinned by an exceptional understanding of basic skills and knowledge. If you don't have high-level knowledge of the basics, you cannot hope to be able to execute any task that is advanced.

To be brilliant at the basics in the military, you must have the discipline to train these skills over and over. Investing is no different. To be brilliant at the basics of investing, you must continue to learn and educate yourself; you must constantly practise skills such as analysis and valuation; and you must ensure that you don't lose your 'brilliance at the basics' or your other skills will also suffer.

Time is a crucial asset for an investor. The more time you have, the greater your returns can compound or the more opportunity you have to recover from a downturn. Time is something that we can't get any more of, so we must use what we have to the best of our ability.

Through discipline, you can begin your journey far sooner than the undisciplined and have maximum ability to create investment returns. Let's take a quick look at the difference between investing $30,000 when you're 30 versus when you're 40 (see figure 2.1). We'll assume a retirement age of 65 and an annual compounding return of 6 per cent.

#### Figure 2.1: Investing at age 30 versus 40

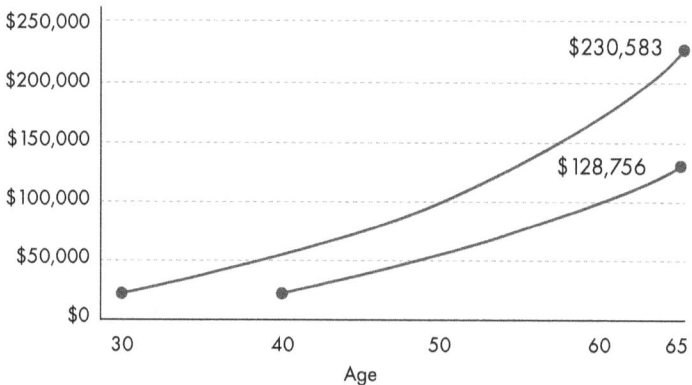

As you can see, by waiting an extra 10 years to invest, you would be over $100,000 worse off at retirement age. This difference is why discipline to invest is so important. Imagine how much better off you would be if you started investing when you were 20. There is a great investing saying: 'The best time to invest was yesterday, the second-best time is today, and the worst time is tomorrow.' We all wish that we could have invested sooner than when we did, but the most important thing is to start today and not tomorrow.

## ASSET CLASSES

Financial freedom is unlikely to be achieved through your employment salary alone. If financial freedom can't be achieved just by working a job, how do we do it? The answer is investing.

Investing can occur through many different asset types. Table 2.1 summarises some of the most common and their respective pros and cons; let's look at them in more detail.

**Table 2.1: Common asset classes and their pros and cons**

| Asset class | Pros | Cons |
|---|---|---|
| Cash | Liquid<br>Risk free | Loses value |
| Bonds | Low risk<br>Low cost of entry | Low return |
| Shares | Liquid<br>Good return<br>Low cost of entry | Highly volatile<br>Difficult to leverage |
| Property | Good return<br>Lower volatility<br>Ability to leverage | Illiquid<br>High cost of entry |

## Cash

Our first asset type is one that everybody is familiar with – cash! Although some people may not realise it, cash is an asset, and it can form the backbone of some people's investment portfolios. The biggest advantage of cash is that it is an extremely liquid asset, which can be important when you require fast access to your investments.

One of the biggest downfalls of cash is that it actually loses value each year due to inflation. This means that if you hide a stack of bills under your mattress, when you come back a few years later, you are not able to buy as much as you could when you originally hid the money. Cash is considered a defensive asset because there is effectively no investment risk, and it will not grow in value the same way other assets can.

## Bonds

Our next asset class is bonds. A bond is a loan, usually to a government or corporation, that will typically pay interest each year and returns your original investment amount at the end of the bond period. Everyday investors will usually invest in Australian Government Bonds because they are usually seen as very close to risk free, as the government is extremely unlikely to be unable to repay the loan. Bonds can sometimes be a complicated concept, so let's give you a quick run-through of the lingo and follow up with an example. Here are some common terms associated with bonds:

- Face value – the amount of money invested.
- Coupon rate – can be thought of as the annual interest rate.
- Maturity date – the date on which the bond will mature, and you will receive back the face value of the bond.

For example: an investor purchases an Australian Government Bond on 11 July 2020 with a face value of $1,000. The bond has a coupon rate of 1 per cent and has a maturity date of 10 July 2025.

In this example, the investor will pay $1,000 to purchase the bond and they will receive $10 of interest every year. On 10 July 2025, the investor will have their original $1,000 returned to them and they will have earned 1 per cent of interest in each of the five years they owned the bond for a total of $50 interest.

As you can see, bonds can be a good low-risk but low-return investment. Returns from bonds have stayed very low over the last decade around the world, which makes it difficult to build a large nest egg through them. Bonds are not as liquid as cash but are still considered a relatively liquid investment. Finally, bonds can deliver a steady and predictable fixed income stream, which is an attractive prospect for some investors who have small investment goals.

## Shares

Shares are one of the most popular asset classes in Australia. A recent 2020 Australian Securities Exchange (ASX) Investor Study indicated that 74 per cent of people who invest in Australia invest in shares. When you purchase a share, you are purchasing an ownership stake in the company whose share you have bought. Naturally, some of these companies may have hundreds of millions of shares, so you are only owning a very small portion of the company.

Some of the reasons that people invest in shares are that shares are a liquid investment that can be sold quickly, there is a lower cost of entry (often only a couple of hundred dollars) and you can often research companies with ease – especially if you use the company's products regularly.

While there are some great advantages to shares, the biggest disadvantage is that they're extremely difficult to leverage. When you purchase shares, you only receive the same value of the amount you invest – for example, if you buy $50,000 of shares, you only receive $50,000 worth of shares. The other big downside to investing in shares is that they're extremely volatile. It is quite common for shares to have substantial up-and-down movements during a single day, let alone over the course of a year. There are plenty of examples of shares that may be up 15 per cent one year and then down 20 per cent the next.

## Property

Our final and most favoured asset class is property. Shelter is an enduring requirement of human beings, which is one of the reasons that property investing allows everyday people to become extremely wealthy. Everybody needs somewhere to live, and this necessity is what underpins the permanent demand for property.

Property investment is extremely powerful for one simple reason: leverage. As we discussed earlier, if you're investing in shares you only receive the value that you put in. Property is the opposite!

When you purchase property, you may only invest $50,000 but you receive an asset that could be worth $500,000. The amazing thing about this situation is that you earn your growth on the $500,000 property and not the $50,000 that you invested. If you earn 10 per cent growth in your first year, you earn $50,000 – not the $5,000 you would have earned on your original investment had you invested in shares. This is a massive $45,000 difference in just a single year.

The other big benefit of investing in property is that it carries significantly less risk for the return you receive. Where shares are extremely volatile and may move up or down by as much as 15 to 20 per cent every year, property is far less volatile in its movements.

While we love property, it would not be fair to the other asset classes if we didn't briefly mention some of the disadvantages. The biggest disadvantage to property is that it is very illiquid. Where it may only take a couple of hours to sell shares, it can take weeks or months to sell property. Of course, this risk can be offset by planning and having buffers in place, but the risk does still exist. The other big downside to property is that it can have a high barrier to entry, which is why discipline is so important in property investing. Direct investment into property will usually require tens of thousands of dollars, and this can sometimes be a challenge for some people to save – often requiring years of discipline and control to enter the market. There are some alternative methods to enter the market faster, and we will discuss those in the next part of this chapter.

Regardless of the downsides, we believe that the benefits of property substantially outweigh the negatives, and that is why we have chosen property as our primary vehicle of wealth creation.

## COMMON METHODS TO INVEST IN PROPERTY

There is no question that the hardest property to purchase is your first one. For many people, particularly those in younger generations, the idea of saving $50,000 to $100,000 for a house deposit is extremely daunting, especially given that wage growth has been quite limited over the last 10 years. This is why discipline is so important – without discipline, it will be even harder to stick to your goal of financial freedom through property.

Although saving for your deposit is the most common method for getting into property, it is not the only way. Let's explore some of the ways that you can invest in property and begin your property-investment journey.

### Save your money

The first and most common method is to save your money. This approach is without a doubt the most difficult and requires the most discipline. Too often we have seen friends and clients spend months saving and then fall off the wagon when they were so close to their first deposit. The new shiny car or the grand and luxurious international holiday was too enticing, and they decided to sacrifice years of hard work.

Those who are disciplined and successful at saving are usually so because they have created a manageable plan. Rome wasn't built in a day, and neither was a healthy savings account. The most important thing to remember is that you need to pay yourself first – you must pay a portion of every single paycheque into your savings first so that you can maintain your savings discipline.

You need to remain pragmatic about saving for a house deposit – this will be a goal that takes years to achieve. People in some Australian capital cities will take an average of five to seven years to save for a deposit, whereas those living in some bigger cities are currently taking 10-plus years.

### Purchase with family/partner

It's a lot of work for one person to save enough money to buy a house in Sydney – why don't we halve it then? If you're struggling to maintain the savings discipline for a housing deposit by yourself, a great alternative is to look at buying with your partner or a family member.

Although this won't be an approach for everyone, if you can purchase a property with a partner or family member, it could dramatically reduce the amount of time it takes for you to break into the market. There are different ways in which you can structure a purchase with another person, but most importantly this route may get you into the market years ahead of where you might be if you went down this road alone.

### Joint venture

A joint venture can be another great option for those looking to get into the property market. A joint venture is simply a deal between two or more people where each person brings different skills/qualifications to the deal. Although purchasing with family or a partner could still technically be considered as a joint venture, a joint venture is typically between people who only have a business relationship – not family or very close friends.

Joint ventures are very common in property development but are also used in more traditional property investment. Usually, people will use a joint venture when they have something to offer but are also missing something that stops them doing a deal. A common example is where somebody has a large deposit but doesn't have any borrowing capacity, so they bring in a joint venture partner who may not have much of a deposit, but has a large borrowing capacity – or vice versa.

### Guarantor

Guarantors are often associated with purchasing an owner-occupier property, but they are still an option for some people for investing. A guarantor is somebody who already owns a property and agrees to let you use their property as a form of collateral with a lender.

Most often, parents will help their children by acting as a guarantor, but it can sometimes be done by very close friends. Guarantors can be a great option because they can reduce the deposit you require, and they can also reduce some of the costs associated with buying a property. Guarantor loans are much less common for property investment, but they are still possible, particularly with the help of great team members, which we will discuss in Step 3 – Teamwork.

### Equity release

An equity release is one of the most powerful tools in a property investor's belt. An equity release can be used when you have another property, such as a principal place of residence or another investment property, and that property has excess equity. The fantastic part about using an equity release is that you don't have to save a cent, because you are using the excess value of the property compared to the debt against it.

An equity release is what helps seasoned property investors continue to purchase properties without having to save a new deposit each time. Equity releases have also become quite common for people who may have bought an owner-occupier home in a capital city that has seen massive growth over the last 10 to 20 years. It's amazing how many of our clients are sitting on a hypothetical goldmine of equity in their homes that they could be using to build a property portfolio.

### Alternative methods

For those of you who love property and know that property is where you want to build your wealth, there are some other avenues for investment. All the previous methods have focused on direct property ownership, but there is another type of ownership available: indirect ownership.

Indirect ownership is where you don't actually own the property, but you own a portion of another asset which owns the property.

The two most common types of indirect property ownership are listed and unlisted property funds.

In Australia, listed property funds are called Australian real estate investment trusts (A-REITs) and they trade on the Australian Securities Exchange (ASX). A-REITs raise money by listing on the stock exchange and people buy shares in their trust. An A-REIT will then use this money to go out and acquire property, often worth hundreds of millions of dollars. As the properties go up in value and the trusts receive rental payments each month, your investment will pay you a dividend and the shares will also rise in value.

So, although this is like buying a share of a company, you are actually buying a share of property and your investment return is still based on the property. This type of real estate exposure is favoured by some people because it is more liquid; since you are buying shares traded on the stock exchange, you can sell your interest in a very short period, unlike traditional property. This can also be a cheaper way to enter the property market because a single share in an A-REIT may only cost a few dollars as opposed to a whole property deposit costing you hundreds of thousands.

An unlisted property fund is very similar to an A-REIT except that it is not listed on the ASX. An unlisted fund will still raise funds to buy property, but it will do so directly from investors rather than through the stock exchange.

### THE INVESTING MINDSET

Mindset is an often-undervalued aspect of a person's success in life. We all have those days where things can feel difficult, but those people who understand and challenge their mindsets are likely to be more successful than others. Discipline underpins a successful mindset, and this is why disciplined people are typically more successful than undisciplined people. Mindset is at the core of all military personnel and the tasks they are often asked to complete. It is even more difficult to spend nine months deployed, away from family and friends, if you do not have a good mindset.

We approach mindset from two initial perspectives: open or closed. If you have an open mindset, we then say you can have two attitudes towards learning and improvement: growth or fixed.

## Open mindset

An open mindset is what everybody should strive to have. It is characterised by a willingness to hear others' ideas, thoughts and perspectives and an understanding that you may not necessarily have all the answers. An open mindset is what allows you to be willing to learn new things and expand on your knowledge, as well as change your own perspective.

Good investors need an open mindset because they will constantly be challenged on their beliefs of what makes a good investment. An open mindset will allow you to know when to invest and when not to invest. It will help you decide if you need to sell an underperforming asset, and it will be the driver behind taking calculated risks when you believe that you have analysed all information available.

## Closed mindset

The opposite to an open mindset is a closed mindset. If you have a closed mindset, you believe that you are always right and that any counter perspective must be wrong. You may not even be willing to hear others' ideas, thoughts or perspectives. Often your beliefs are not rooted in reality; however, your closed mindset leads you to believe that you are always correct.

A closed mindset can be extremely detrimental to an investor because it will likely lead to bad decision-making. A closed mindset may lead you to believe in the investment prospects of a location for false reasons, and you are likely to be unwilling to adjust your perspective. It can also lead you to continue to hold very bad investments just because you ultimately believe you are always right, despite evidence highlighting that you are not.

### Growth perspective

A person with an open mindset and a growth perspective is the ideal investor persona. An open mindset highlights your willingness to have your own views challenged, and a growth perspective demonstrates that you are willing to then learn from these different views.

Investors with a growth perspective are primed to achieve the best results. By adding a growth perspective to your open mindset, you will be able to have your views challenged and then learn from the new knowledge that has been presented. This means that in future scenarios, you will be able to implement this new knowledge rather than repeating similar past mistakes.

### Fixed perspective

While an open mindset is a great start, a fixed perspective will still see you operating at a suboptimal level. If you have a fixed perspective, you are willing to listen to others' ideas, thoughts and opinions, but ultimately will not learn from or adopt the experiences. This is especially damaging if you are shown new and innovative ways to approach an investment but still choose to utilise your original and less effective methods.

## HAVING A STRATEGIC PLAN

In the military, planning is divided up into three unique and critical realms: the tactical, operational and strategic fields (see figure 2.2). The tactical realm belongs to soldiers, sailors and airmen and airwomen who are deployed on the battlefield and are actively in the fight. These personnel are given a specific mission in order to achieve an objective set by commanders and planners. Tactical missions may last a few days or weeks, depending on the nature of the mission.

Figure 2.2: Tactical, operational and strategic planning

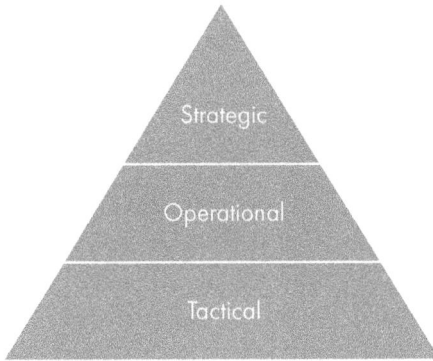

| | Military planning | Investment property planning |
|---|---|---|
| **Strategic** ↑ | The level where the nation's overarching strategy is determined by senior leaders. Resources are allocated to achieve the strategic end state. | Determining your overall property portfolio goals and defining your version of financial freedom. Setting your overall timeline to achieve your property goals. |
| **Operational** ↑ | The level where campaigns are planned and implemented to achieve strategic objectives in theatre. | Planning how many acquisitions (and what types) will be required to achieve your version of financial freedom. Setting two to three medium-term goals so you can track your progress. |
| **Tactical** ↑ | The level where tactical engagement is planned and executed to achieve certain military objectives in line with the efforts of the campaign. | Setting budgets, undertaking market research, reducing expenses and saving for deposits. Setting timeframes until your next purchase to ensure continued progress. |

The level above tactical is operational. Operational planners will assess and enact the campaign as a whole, part of which includes how many tactical missions will help achieve the desired outcome for the entire operation. Operational campaigns can last months if not years, but all tactical missions are planned in a way that advances the operational goal overall.

Lastly, the strategic realm is where multiple operational campaigns are planned out to determine whether the nation's overarching goals and interests are being achieved and defended. There is no end to strategic planning – priorities will simply change over time, and the operational and tactical realms will shift and adapt to prioritise and achieve the new desired end state.

Without the strategic outlook, the operational campaigns and tactical missions are pointless and will lack direction. Military members on the ground will be conducting missions without a true goal. Without a strategic end state in mind, personnel and resources will be assigned to missions for no real purpose, and this often results in unacceptable levels of risk being adopted. Each of the realms requires a different but important level of discipline. Discipline ranges from the short periods on the tactical level through to years for the strategic level.

This is the same approach to discipline that is required in property investment. A single deal requires the discipline to assess and manage the acquisition process, while your overall portfolio goal will require years of discipline to ensure you continue moving in the correct direction.

Let's look at an example of strategic, operational and tactical planning in property investing. Antonio and Maria both want to commit to their property-investing journey over the next few years. After planning their desired end state, they decide that their strategic goal will be to gain a passive income that is substantial enough to allow them both to quit their jobs and have more time to spend with their children and wider family. This is their version of financial freedom and therefore their strategic end state.

To achieve this, Antonio and Maria set themselves an operational-level goal that requires them to build a four-property portfolio over the next 10 years. They assess that this goal is achievable for them, and once the properties are fully paid off, they will be able to provide the income that Antonio and Maria need to live comfortably. This level of planning helps Antonio and Maria identify the objectives they need to secure to achieve their goal, while breaking down their broader strategic goal into four individual operations (or purchases) – making planning and preparation easier.

On a tactical level, Antonia and Maria know that they need to make several changes to their daily spending habits. Tactical actions they decide to implement include reducing the amount of takeaway food and cafe coffees that they both buy, and to redirect more of their savings into an account that's set aside for house deposits. They also decide to reduce their budget for their annual holidays and refinance their mortgage so they can reduce their interest paid, to direct more funds towards their next house deposit. As we've said before, small actions when compounded can create great results when implemented properly.

This is why we stress that it's critical to have a strategic plan for your personal investments and finances. Without a strategic goal in mind, the tactics and operations required to purchase properties won't necessarily build to anything. Whether your strategic intent involves building a flow of passive income that will one day substitute your working wage, like Antonio's and Maria's, or purchasing properties that have considerable capital growth so you can sell them for substantial profits later in life, you need to have a strategic plan in place so you can buy assets that will help you achieve these goals. If you don't have an end state in mind, you could find yourself buying entirely wrong properties for the goals you want to achieve.

This can set you back years in your investing journey, all because you didn't take the time to plan the goals that you envisioned for yourself.

Some examples of overarching strategies that you may choose to enact for your own investing journey include:

- attaining a positive cash flow
- focusing on capital growth
- choosing properties with cosmetic renovation or subdivision potential
- knock down and rebuild
- buying off-the-plan properties
- commercial investing.

No matter what your strategy is, as long as you have conducted your research and ensured that your strategy will help you achieve your goals, you'll have direction and purpose in your investing journey.

## HOW MARGINAL IMPROVEMENTS CAN MAKE A BIG IMPACT

The term 'aggregation of marginal gains' originated from a now renowned British cyclist performance director, Dave Brailsford, who trained the British cycling team from 2003. After 100 years of ordinary performance from the team, Brailsford introduced a new strategy to the training program. His strategy was to seek and attain just 1 per cent improvement in every area that the team could find, each day. The team began to seek improvement in obvious areas, such as physical training and development, but also began to search for improvements in smaller, previously overlooked areas. Minuscule changes included testing and adjusting each rider's personal sleeping arrangements such as pillows to ensure that the riders achieved optimal sleep. Even the colour of each rider's bike was changed to white so the team could more easily spot any dust particles or imperfections that could cause the smallest changes to the bike's overall performance.

In just 10 years, through overwhelming and consistent discipline, Brailsford's strategy won the British cycling team 178 world championships, 66 gold medals across the Olympics and Paralympics and five Tour de France victories. This was all achieved by dedicated and disciplined individuals who actively integrated the smallest changes every day to attain remarkable results.

Figure 2.3 depicts the aggregation of marginal gains.

**Figure 2.3: The power of marginal gains**

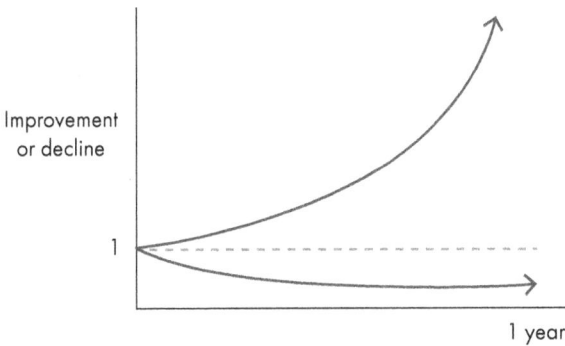

Although the aggregation of marginal gains can be implemented to achieve success, the opposite phenomenon is one through which you can quickly find yourself in a position of failure. Lack of discipline is one reason why so many people consistently demonstrate poor financial habits throughout their lives and rarely put money aside for investing, let alone an emergency fund. This can quickly result in marginal decline as opposed to marginal gains. For some investors, it can be all too easy to find themselves in a position where their financial habits and education disintegrate at 1 per cent a day, without them even being aware of it. These people can end up living paycheque to paycheque until they hit a financial speedbump that their working wage simply can't fix.

We have witnessed some of these people spiralling into a personal financial crisis because of the decisions they have made. Inevitably, they end up turning to credit cards and short-term loans with sky-high interest rates to dig themselves out of the huge hole of debt they spent themselves into. These types of financial mistakes can take many years to reverse, even if you implement a healthy budget and remediate spending habits. And for every year that you are paying off debt, that's another year of investing opportunity lost.

This is not where anyone wants or needs to be financially, and this is not the future that any person would aspire to for themselves or their families. Setting financial goals and being money savvy is challenging, but believe us when we say that living in consumer debt (also known as bad debt) in your 20s or surviving on the Age Pension in your 70s will be so much harder.

This highlights the importance of continuously manifesting discipline and consistency throughout the duration of your financial journey. As you grow, you'll be surrounded by friends, family, acquaintances and work colleagues on their own paths. There will be times when you will be tempted to follow the same spending habits as these people, even if they are earning substantially more or less than you. Trust us when we say that we understand how tempting it is to spend your paycheque on drinks, takeaway food, holidays and exciting experiences, especially when all the people around you seem to be consistently splurging.

This is why it is crucial to set your own budget and financial boundaries and have the discipline to stick to them, even in social situations or in the face of peer pressure. Of course, there is always room for fun – that is why we encourage healthy and sustainable budgeting. Just like dieting, your financial budget should set you up for success while allowing you to treat yourself to fun experiences. But if your discretionary spending has begun to outweigh your savings and investment accounts, this should be your personal amber warning signal. We can guarantee that a fourth cocktail at dinner or that third ski trip for the year with friends won't be nearly as satisfying as settlement day for your next investment property!

# Step 3:
# TEAMWORK

From day one of initial training, recruits are taught that the force of many will always outweigh the force of one. From military drill practice to room inspections, the team must work together to succeed. If one person makes a wrong drill movement on the parade square, or if one member doesn't fold their socks in the correct way, the whole team fails. If the team doesn't win together, no-one wins at all. This means that the team must work to exceptional levels at all times and help other team members in order to win. This instils a strong sense of teamwork in the military and creates of culture of 'leaving no man behind'. This reminds us of one of our favourite quotes: 'If you want to go fast, go alone, but if you want to go far, go together.' Nothing in life has taught us the value of teamwork quite like the military. The property game is no different: teamwork is absolutely crucial to your overall success.

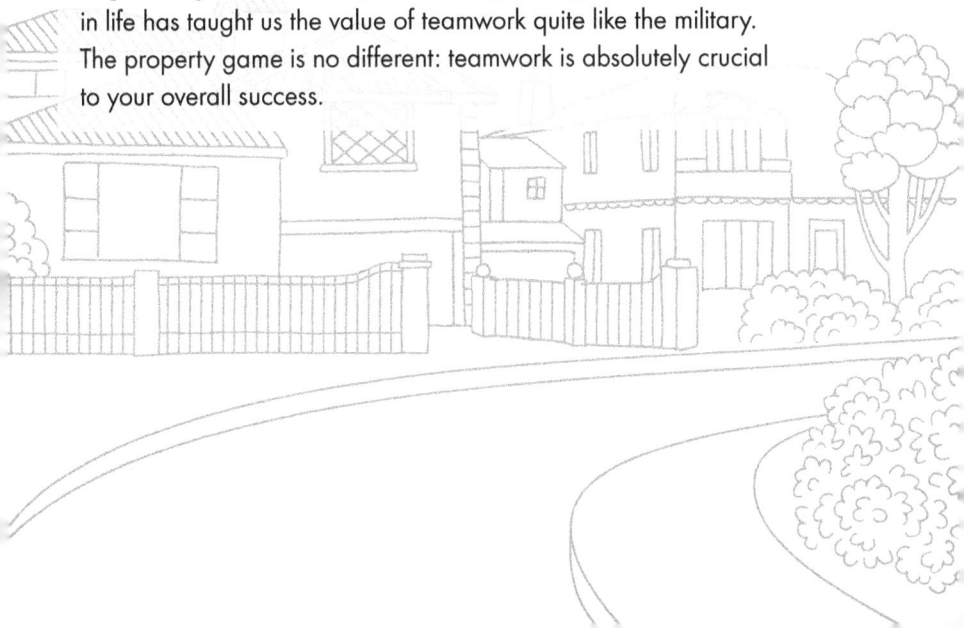

Step 1: Reveille

Step 2: Discipline

**Step 3: Teamwork**

Step 4: Professional mastery

Step 5: Excellence

Step 6: Mission analysis

Step 7: Courage

Step 8: Adaptability and flexibility

Step 9: Dedication

Step 10: Loyalty

## Step 3: Teamwork

Building your support team for your property journey will be key to your success and is essential if your goal is to achieve financial freedom. At the time of writing this book, we can count eight members on our trusted property portfolio team. We've built this team over the years as we realised that we couldn't take on our property-investing journey alone. We have a trusted accountant, solicitor, mortgage broker, property managers, buyer's agents (before we created Atlas Property Group) and, of course, incredible family, friends and each other. We are going to highlight the importance of each and every one of the these team members and help you understand why you absolutely need to have a working body of professionals on your side as you progress through your own property journey.

### YOU CAN'T KNOW IT ALL

Why do you need to build a team? For one simple reason: you can't know everything about everything. Just like a fully trained medical doctor will need a mechanic if their car breaks down, and a lawyer might need a plumber if a drain bursts in the middle of the night, investors are no exception to the rule. Being a successful investor takes research, time, education and effort. However, the best investors know their limitations and understand the value of outsourcing to experts in their fields.

You might be familiar with the quote, 'Do what you do best and outsource the rest.' We emulate this mantra because you cannot be the best at everything. There are investors who have committed countless hours to researching, analysing and self-teaching their way through the market in order to independently move through their own property journey. This is no easy feat and these investors should be highly commended for their efforts; however, if you have a busy lifestyle, family, full-time job, school or university commitments or other considerable obligations, we highly recommend this team-based approach for you. It will save you money and time, and it is also likely to save you from making mistakes along the way.

In the military, teams are made up of specialist operators with unique and well-practised skill sets. Teamwork at its finest is exhibited every day in the military through teams of diverse people. To launch a single fighter aircraft off the tarmac and into the air, a significant number of individuals need to come together and work towards a common goal. These people range from logisticians to electrical engineers, intelligence analysts to air traffic control, ground crew to airfield security. No-one is expected to do it all, and the pilot certainly knows that without their trusted team no aircraft can take off. This is why military personnel train to be excellent in their field of expertise – because everyone is relying upon one another to get the job done. All in all, the efforts of many outweigh the efforts of one, and when the team works together, the team's performance will consistently outperform the efforts of a singular person.

So, what team members do we recommend you have on your trusted team? We're going to unpack some of the most common professionals that every property investor should investigate.

## ACCOUNTANT

You may think that accountants are only required by people who have multimillion-dollar investment portfolios or have so many properties that they simply can't keep track of them by themselves. We're here to tell you that having an accountant on your side can help you smartly build your property portfolio from day one and make the most of your tax return every financial year.

For those who are just starting out on their property journey, this is a fantastic opportunity for you to engage with an accountant to begin setting up your ideal investment structure. Due to your personal circumstances or family arrangements, an accountant may recommend several routes for how to purchase your property in the most effective manner. They may recommend that you set up a trust in order to maintain separation between your personal name and the assets you own (which becomes significantly more important as you continue to grow your portfolio). Accountants may also recommend that your significant other should purchase the property in their name because you already have too much 'good' or 'bad' debt. Good debt is debt that assists you to purchase appreciating assets such as investment properties or investment loans. Bad debt is debt that is used to finance depreciating assets and can include things like car loans or credit cards.

Regardless of your personal situation, an accountant will act as your trusted expert and provide you with the best establishment advice for your personal circumstances. If you structure your wealth smartly from the beginning, it will save you a lot of pain in the future.

Accountants can also help you navigate the complex Australian taxation system for property investors. Accountants are experts in knowing what you can and cannot claim on tax for your investment property. Better yet, accountants will also provide you with expert advice on how you can minimise your tax liability so you can keep more cash in your pocket at the end of every financial year.

Some investors may feel comfortable (or stubborn) enough to manage their own taxes and would prefer to save the few hundred dollars that a qualified accountant will charge to manage the burden for them. However, we advocate that every wise investor should have their own accountant, because they are the expert in maximising your portfolio returns and your tax return, and keeping you out of financial trouble when tax law enters a 'grey area'. Plus, some accountants will help you lower your tax liability and help you find additional items that you can claim on tax, which instantly offsets their fee – which is often also a tax deduction!

## MORTGAGE BROKER

Mortgage brokers are key team players that we receive a lot of questions about from our clients. We support the use of mortgage brokers for similar reasons as to why we recommend an accountant. Mortgage brokers are specialists in loans, and they work with their clients to find them a loan that best suits their needs. As a property investor, your perfect loan will likely be a combination of strategic lender choice (to maximise your future capacity for additional investment loans), competitive interest rates and favourable loan terms.

A mortgage broker can provide you with several key advantages. First, as a property investor, you may want to maximise your borrowing capacity so you can buy a property in your desired price range. If you have a complicated payslip, existing loans, credit cards or multiple sources of income, your mortgage broker can help you navigate through the plethora of home loans out there to find one which suits your circumstances. If a lender gives you a certain borrowing capacity that is not quite the figure you were hoping for, your broker can provide you with actionable steps to achieve the highest borrowing capacity possible.

Once you've found a loan that suits your needs, your broker will liaise with the lender and help you fill out all of the necessary paperwork. This will assist you during the settlement journey, once you've found your perfect property. All in all, finding and securing the perfect loan is time consuming at the best of times. Having a trusted specialist who knows how to read your personal financial situation and work effectively with lenders can save you time, money and stress. The more time you have on your side as a property buyer, the better.

Mortgage brokers earn their money through recommending bank loans and products to their clients. Once the clients sign on to a loan, the broker typically receives a commission from the bank. Some mortgage brokers do charge their clients fees, but we generally utilise the services of brokers who receive their commission from the banks.

Often our clients raise concerns about mortgage brokers only utilising loans from particular lenders because they may receive a higher commission. We are here to tell you that this a very common misconception. While there are differences in commissions that a broker may receive, this difference is often only a few hundred dollars. Brokers are far more incentivised to send a client to a lender that they know will approve the loan and receive a slightly smaller commission rather than chasing the bigger commissions and having clients rejected by lenders.

Some investors choose not to utilise a mortgage broker since brokers can't work with every lender available. If you want to have access to every lender and every home loan in existence, mortgage brokers may not be for you. However, we recommend thinking carefully about whether you have the time to assess every home loan on its merits. Do you want to spend your days liaising with every lender possible in order to secure the highest borrowing capacity? Probably not. You're an investor – you have market research to do. You might have a full-time job or other commitments. That's why we trust our loans with a loan expert, and we think that you should do the same.

## BUYER'S AGENT

If you were the captain of a ship, your buyer's agent (BA) would be your second in command – your right-hand person. The BA is arguably the most important member of a property investor's team. BAs are qualified, licensed property experts who have years of experience in the property industry. They have a strong understanding of the market, are able to identify high-performing properties in thriving suburbs and can evaluate the merits of properties that could possess outstanding investment potential.

Since property is a BA's bread and butter, they have access to data repositories and services that provide market insights that aren't accessible to investors without extremely expensive annual fees.

BAs use these repositories to access key market data. Some of this data includes:

- extended time series of suburb data to analyse trends
- expert market commentary and outlooks
- graphical representations of data to use for the client's reference
- segmented data for a specific range of properties (for example, sales data for four bedroom homes in a suburb, rather than just aggregated data on all homes in general).

In addition to data repositories and market experience, BAs also have access to industry partners and connections. A BA will typically have their own team of trusted partners, including accountants, real estate agents, solicitors, financial planners, mortgage brokers and more. This provides the BA with trusted industry partners who they can refer their own clients to in order to secure a swift and smooth settlement. If a BA has worked with these partners before, they can trust that they'll give their clients a professional and seamless experience, which becomes crucial once the property's settlement date approaches. BAs also use their real estate partners to access off-market deals. Off-market deals can be a great way to secure a property below market price. If you're seeking off-market opportunities, you'll certainly want a trusted BA paired with a great real estate agent on your side.

As for further education, researching your BA's background will be beneficial. You wouldn't trust a doctor without a medical degree, just like you wouldn't trust an accountant without an accounting degree. While a BA may only need a vocational education to qualify as a certified BA, a relevant tertiary education (a bachelor's or master's degree) will highlight to you their ability to analyse situations and think critically about investing and your property journey. Ultimately, the background and experience that a BA has delivered to their clients is their most important selling point, but understanding their educational qualifications will give you an insight into their abilities to advocate on your behalf in the property industry. Not every BA will have a qualification in this area, but experience in the property industry is a must. As with every other member on your team, ensure your do your research to increase the likelihood that you find the right BA for you.

## SOLICITOR/CONVEYANCER

A solicitor or conveyancer is the professional that will handle all of the legal aspects of buying an investment property on your behalf. Conveyancers strictly deal with property law in transactions, whereas solicitors are well-versed in all areas of law and therefore have a full understanding of all legal elements involved in purchasing property. Since solicitors have a broader knowledge of law, they are able to provide a more holistic assessment of your property contract.

A solicitor is of paramount importance when it comes to evaluating the contract for sale. They will ensure that the contract is written fairly, is within the law and isn't written in such a way that it disproportionately favours the vendor. They will also ensure that the contract for sale accurately describes the property and will assess the covenants and easements. This information regarding the property is often found within land titles, which are best analysed by a professional who knows exactly what they're looking for.

As well as your accountant, your solicitor will ensure that your legal structures (if you are buying through a trust or company) are correctly established and executed. Once it comes time for the exchange of contracts, your solicitor will act on your behalf with the vendor's solicitor to ensure that the exchange goes smoothly and settlement is achieved on time.

## REAL ESTATE AGENT

Real estate agents sell properties on behalf of the owners. Even as a property investor, having a positive relationship with the seller's advocate is paramount. Real estate agents frequently deal with unqualified, unmotivated and illegitimate buyers, which can make it hard for everyday investors to be taken seriously. Given this, it's absolutely critical to establish yourself as a motivated professional through the eyes of the real estate agent as early as possible. Agents want to work with truly interested and qualified buyers, not time wasters who do not invest the effort to conduct their own research and due diligence. Some buyers may choose to have their interests represented by an experienced professional such as a BA, who deals with real estate agents every day of the week.

It is important to note that, depending on which state you are in, real estate agents only have a fiduciary duty to the seller – not the buyer. That is, the real estate agent has a legal responsibility to sell the property with the owner's best interests in the forefront of their mind. This is why having a BA on your side is so important.

Real estate agents are experts in the suburbs that they work within. If you have certain requirements or are looking for a particular type of property, real estate agents will be able to help you narrow your search and should be able to refer relevant listings to you.

An important thing to keep in mind is that the real estate agent will be looking to close a deal quickly and at a price point that is in the vendor's best interests. As an investor, make sure you always do your own research or have your BA do the legwork for you. Securing a property at the right price (preferably below market value) is one of the first steps to securing a successful investment property. Always ensure you complete the necessary due diligence on the property before entering negotiations with the real estate agent.

Similar to all relationships in property, if you have a positive relation-ship with the real estate agent, chances are they will assist you with all of your property-related questions and help ensure an easy jour-ney to settlement. Excellent relationships can even result in access to off-market opportunities, especially if you have the help of a BA.

## PROPERTY MANAGER

Property managers are specialists in managing investment properties on behalf of the owner. Property managers usually charge a percentage fee of your property's rental income in exchange for their management services. Typical property management services include:

- hosting inspections for prospective renters
- assessing rental applications to find a suitable tenant
- managing rental income and property-related expenses
- providing rental income statements for your records
- arranging any repairs that the property may require on your behalf.

In the worst circumstances, a property manager can also represent you in mediation or tribunals if legal problems arise with your tenant (such as if the tenant damages the property and refuses to repair it, or refuses to pay their rent).

High-performing property managers are worth their weight in gold. As we will discuss in more depth later, property investing should be low maintenance. If you're doing it right, you shouldn't be spending more than 10 hours on management per property per year. If you're spending more time than that, you need to revaluate your portfolio management strategy. If you have a full-time job or family and life commitments, you need to be able to manage your portfolio in a time-effective way. If you don't, you run the risk of becoming overly involved in your portfolio and exhausting yourself – which will deter you from building a portfolio that is big enough to provide you with the financial freedom that you seek. Property managers help you with this process – they are the experts in seamless management processes. Engaging with one will save you time, money and stress in the long run. Plus, like many of your team members' services, their rates may be a tax deduction from your portfolio expenses.

## FINANCIAL PLANNER

A financial planner is your personal finance expert. Financial planners specialise in assessing your personal financial situation and building a step-by-step plan for you to achieve your financial goals. They can provide advice on things like:

- building a retirement plan
- paying down your home loan faster
- creating a passive income investment strategy
- structuring your wealth for future generations
- balancing your money across a variety of investments and asset classes.

No matter your financial goals, a financial planner is your go-to team member.

You can engage a financial planner for a short amount of time to achieve a short-term financial goal, or for an ongoing period to formulate and execute a personalised strategic plan. Financial planners will be able to assess your priorities, assets, debts, income, expenses and estate plans to recommend a path forward. We recommend financial planners to anyone who sees value in having a money mentor.

A financial planner may recommend a range of asset classes you can invest in, depending on your available equity, personal circumstances and risk-tolerance level. For example, they may recommend a variety of domestic or international stocks with high growth potential for a young person who has a high risk tolerance and time on their side for multiple market cycles. For an older investor, a financial planner may recommend a low-risk managed fund or government bonds, so that their retirement fund remains invested but in very low-risk products.

A financial planner, in conjunction with your accountant, can also recommend tax-effective strategies on how to minimise your tax obligations. This can be the make-or-break aspect of your personal property-investment journey, particularly given the complicated nature of the Australian taxation system.

Once your financial planner has evaluated your situation and desired end state, your planner will develop and present a statement of advice. This statement provides an overview of your current financial state, your risk-tolerance level, suggested investments and their fees, and the pros and cons of other investment types.

## TOWN PLANNER

If you're a property developer (or would like to be!), a town planner is a critical subject-matter expert that you need onside. If you're only interested in investing in pre-established property, a town planner won't be entirely necessary, but they can provide advice on any renovations or improvements that you plan on making to the property that may require council approval.

For the property developers out there, a town planner will be able to transform your idea into a strategic plan that gains the approval of the local council. Running your ideas past a town planner is the best way to ensure that your vision for a block is feasible before investing all of your hard-earned cash.

Property developing involves a whole specialised team in addition to your pre-established property team due to its increased level of risk and complexity. If you're a developer, you must ensure you conduct the appropriate research and arm yourself with a team that has experience in the development industry.

## FAMILY AND FRIENDS

If you're already in the investing game, you may have discovered that property investing isn't necessarily a thrilling conversation starter at a party. If you're lucky, your family and friends will be enthusiastic and supportive of your journey. However, some of your loved ones simply won't be – whether it be out of disinterest, jealousy, spite or a lack of dedication to their own personal and financial growth. Let us be the first to tell you: not everyone in your life will be supportive of your commitment.

If you're lucky enough to have a robust support base, family and trusted friends can be a great source of support in more ways than one. Positive family and friends play a key role in providing encouragement and advice as you undertake your investment journey. This can be crucial, since the journey to financial freedom can take a long time and be full of speedbumps along the way. A reassuring and positive support network can help you remain focused on your goal and can give you a pat on the back after you've achieved a milestone.

In some cases, as we mentioned in Step 1 – Reveille, family and friends can also act as guarantors, which can help you kickstart your property journey. A guarantor provides a guarantee to the lender that the buyer can be trusted to make all of the appropriate loan repayments in a timely manner. Guarantors often provide their own assets as collateral for the lender in the event that the buyer cannot repay their debts. A guarantor may be advantageous for those who have a smaller deposit than required for the purchase but want to break into the real estate market as soon as possible. This isn't the route for everyone, but it is an option that you may consider.

Conversely, it's likely that not all of your family members and friends will support your journey – particularly given Australia's culture of tall poppy syndrome. The tall poppy is one that rises above the others to strive for better. After a period of growth, this poppy is inevitably cut down to be the same size as the others. Take it from two people who have experienced both support and negativity – you need to reject this culture. You must continue to strive for excellence and push yourself to be better. This doesn't negate the need for modesty in success, but it does abolish the concept of following the crowd and continuing to participate in the rat-race of everyday life. Have the courage to travel against the crowd and talk about your investing journey with your family and friends. Develop your own opinion and education foundation, and remember: if your crowd isn't supportive of your decisions, find a new crowd. Achieving financial freedom will take a lifetime of dedication, education and commitment, and won't be achieved without finding a group of peers and supporters.

To succeed in the property game, you need to have a competent, supportive and trusted team; but your team can't be expected to work unless you do. Once you've found team members that you think will be a good fit, ensure you invest time and effort into these relationships. The best business relationships are those that are built over time where both parties invest effort to make it work. If you stay in contact and put effort into your teambuilding, your chances of success in the property-investing world will multiply tenfold.

# Step 4:
# PROFESSIONAL MASTERY

Every soldier, sailor, airman and airwoman is taught a very specific set of skills that is important on its own, but becomes crucial to the mission's success when combined with their colleagues' skills. Professional mastery is the constant pursuit of perfection of these professionals' skill sets. While true professional mastery can never be attained, the drive to continue learning and improving their mastery of their chosen skill set is its premise.

Step 1: Reveille

Step 2: Discipline

Step 3: Teamwork

**Step 4: Professional mastery**

Step 5: Excellence

Step 6: Mission analysis

Step 7: Courage

Step 8: Adaptability and flexibility

Step 9: Dedication

Step 10: Loyalty

## Step 4: Professional mastery

As we're sure that you're seeing, many of the skills needed to be an excellent military professional are also those needed for success in property investing. While the implementation of these skills may change, the knowledge and ideas that underpin them have a wide variety of uses. Like most things, the more you know and practise a set of skills, the better you will be able to implement them. Whether you're a soldier with a perfect aim, a lawyer who can expertly argue in a courtroom or a property professional who can see the value in deals where others can't, professional mastery is crucial for your future success. By having an expert mastery of the basics of property and property investment, you will be well on your path to professional mastery and the financial success that comes with it.

### A HISTORY OF PROPERTY IN AUSTRALIA

Property and property investing has been a much-loved part of Australian life for many decades. Today, property investing is seen as a mainstream activity that many people take part in; however, it wasn't always like that! Property and property investing has experienced many changes over the years, particularly in the past 20 to 30 years. Before we take you through the history, let's first look at why it's important to have this context as a property investor.

Winston Churchill, former Prime Minister of the United Kingdom, once said: 'Those that fail to learn from history are doomed to repeat it.' While the conditions that we live in today are very different to those in the 1980s and 1990s, there are still lessons that we can learn from these decades, when economic conditions and property investing looked starkly different to today.

In the late 1980s and early 1990s, Australia experienced a recession that sent interest rates to astronomical highs of over 17 per cent per annum. While house prices looked very different back then compared with today, we still can't imagine having to pay 17 per cent interest every single year – can you? What is even scarier is that people were paying 17 per cent regardless of whether they were an owner-occupier or investor. At least investors were receiving rental income to help ease the repayment burden!

While it is very unlikely that we will see interest rates return to these levels, what we can take away is that money is currently the cheapest it has ever been. Other than remaining where we are today, there is nowhere rates can go but up. While it might look like a fantastic opportunity to purchase property and only pay a 2 per cent interest rate, savvy investors will ensure they factor in an interest rate buffer for when rates eventually do rise. With long-term interest rates hovering between 5 and 7 per cent, analysing your cash flow and ensuring that you can withstand rates moving back to these levels is a very important aspect of building a strong but sustainable portfolio.

While many people around Australia now invest in property, this wasn't always the case. Although property investing has long been recognised as an effective, efficient and relatively less risky method of investing, there were substantially less people investing in the 1990s compared to today. In 1993, it was estimated that there were around 750,000 Australians who held investments in real estate, representing approximately 6 per cent of the adult population. Thanks to a few factors including greater access to information, lower cost of debt and availability of credit, this number has now swelled to over 2.2 million Australians; but, more importantly, this now accounts for almost 12 per cent of the adult population.

So, what can this change in investor behaviour teach us moving into the future? Well, as we learned in Step 1 – Reveille, the best time to invest was yesterday, the second-best time to invest is today and the worst time to invest is tomorrow. The data doesn't lie: the number of investors has grown rapidly and there is no reason to expect that this will change over the next 30 years.

In their simplest form, property prices and property growth are a function of supply and demand. When demand is greater than supply, prices will grow as more people compete over a smaller pool of properties. This is also backed up by the price growth across all major capital cities over the last 30 years, which can be seen in table 4.1.

*Table 4.1: Property price growth since 1990*

| City | Median price (1990) | Median price (2021) | Growth |
|---|---|---|---|
| Canberra | $120,750 | $859,600 | 612% |
| Melbourne | $131,000 | $930,000 | 610% |
| Hobart | $82,000 | $570,000 | 595% |
| Sydney | $194,000 | $1,200,000 | 519% |
| Adelaide | $97,200 | $576,200 | 493% |
| Perth | $101,125 | $563,000 | 457% |
| Brisbane | $113,000 | $620,000 | 449% |
| Darwin | $101,500 | $525,150 | 417% |

While it might be hard to believe that property values could grow by four or five times over the next 30 years, we doubt that people in the 1990s would have believed that the median price in Sydney would grow to over $1,000,000 by 2021. We don't have a crystal ball to be able to look at values in the next 30 years, but history is a great teacher. We would be wise to listen to the lessons of the past so that we can benefit financially in the future.

## THE PROPERTY CYCLE

The property cycle is an investing concept that helps describe the way properties move up and down in value over time. Understanding the property cycle is crucial, whether you're a potential developer trying to determine the best time to begin your development or an investor wanting to understand how rental values and yields change over time. The property cycle is often represented as a clock, as per figure 4.1.

Although the property cycle uses words like 'decline' or 'bottom' or 'slump', it's important to remember that the values don't necessarily follow a perfectly cyclical path. What this means is that when an area reaches the slumping stage, values are not likely to dip 10 or 20 per cent in value. The practical scenario is that values will often experience long periods of neutral or small growth, such as rises and falls of 1 per cent or 2 per cent. It's a common misconception that the property cycle means that values must always decline at some point, but it's actually much more likely to see a long stagnation before short periods of large growth to reach the top of the market again. A property may move through the entire cycle in as few as six or seven years, but depending on economic conditions, this can extend as far as 12 or 13 years. On average, property owners are likely to see their property complete one full cycle in nine to 11 years.

### Figure 4.1: The property cycle

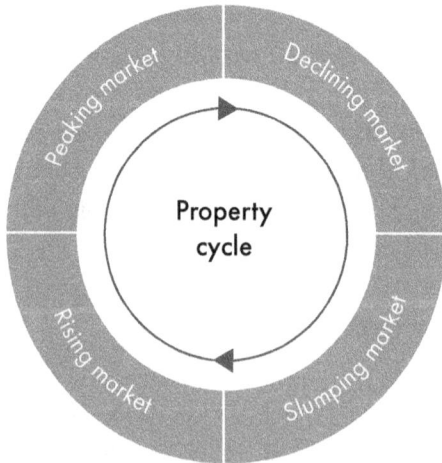

We're going to break down the clock into quarters and describe some of the most common attributes of each stage. Although we're going to discuss it in quarters, the cycle can be broken down as far as each 'hour' of the clock for the technically advanced and economically minded investor.

### Declining market – 12 o'clock to 3 o'clock

The declining market begins immediately after the market peak at 12 o'clock. The declining market signifies that properties have now reached their peak value in the current market and will now begin their decline and/or stagnation in price. The media will begin sporadic reporting of issues within the wider property market and consumer sentiment will begin softening. At this stage of the cycle, you can expect to see a fall in rental yields as prices and rents are mismatched due to the rapid price growth that was experienced during the peak. As property prices start to stagnate or experience minor drops, supply will slowly begin to outpace demand. This will also be reflected by days on market rising as vendors take slightly longer to sell their properties.

### Slumping market – 3 o'clock to 6 o'clock

The slumping market signifies that the decline and/or stagnation in property values has become more widespread and accelerated. At this stage, the media will be consistently reporting on the decline of property and consumer sentiment will be at or approaching its lowest point. At this stage of the cycle, you can expect to see a noticeable fall in formal property valuations, mainly due to the significant levels of supply relative to buyer demand. It will be common for prospective purchasers to have multiple properties to choose from, which will be aided by significant vendor discounting to ensure that they are able to sell their property. Days on market will have risen to their highest levels and you may see properties taking many months to sell. The construction industry will become less profitable as prices fall, and there may be a reduction in the value of goods and services that are related to construction.

### Rising market – 6 o'clock to 9 o'clock

The rising market signifies that property has now reached the bottom of the cycle and will begin to rise. Unfortunately, this can be one of the trickiest times in the cycle because, even if all the measures are indicating a rising market, it is very common for a market to remain 'stuck' in this phase. This can be detrimental for investors who believe they are investing in a rising market, but the market remains stagnant for much longer than anticipated. An excellent example of this was Brisbane in 2010 to 2020 – the city was stuck in the 6 o'clock to 9 o'clock phase of the cycle for much of this time, despite showing many of the fundamental signs that would normally indicate that a market is set to rise and then peak.

In a rising market, media outlets will begin to publish sporadic positive commentary and consumer sentiment will begin to rise. Rental values will start to increase and, while it is still affordable to rent, people will look to 'try before they buy' (that is, rent in an area before making the commitment to buy). Despite this, there will also be a noticeable yet minor increase in sales volumes as those people who like the area look to take advantage of the lower cost of entry. This will also translate into a stabilisation of days on market, which will then begin to trend lower as the market moves closer to the 9 o'clock position. Construction and building will also rise as large developers look to cash in on the lower cost of entry and the anticipation of greater values once their developments are completed. Vendor discounting will still occur; however, it will happen less as the market continues to heat up.

### Peaking market – 9 o'clock to 12 o'clock

The peaking market is arguably the most exciting phase of the cycle for investors. The peaking market signifies that property prices are growing rapidly and will imminently reach their peak in the current cycle. At this stage, the media will be making consistent positive reports on the property market and consumer confidence will be at its highest point. This phase of the cycle is characterised by extreme buyer demand but limited supply. This then forces would-be buyers to pay considerably more to secure a property. This will be reflected in the days on market as properties sell at record speeds. In the early stages of this phase, affordability becomes a major driver as people will typically pay a similar or slightly greater amount of money to rent versus mortgage costs to buy. Property valuations will continue to rise as properties continue to set sales records, and the higher volume of sales consistently provides higher benchmarks for future property sales. The construction and building industries are at maximum capacity as they take advantage of the insatiable demand for property through large developments such as estates or high-rise apartments. Vendor discounting is rarely seen as vendors can choose from multiple offers and properties will frequently sell for more than the asking price.

## PROPERTY PORTFOLIO LIFECYCLE

The property portfolio lifecycle (PPL) is an important concept for property investors and is used to illustrate the different stages in your portfolio journey. By understanding where you are in your journey, you can create structured goals and plans to achieve the next stage in the lifecycle. There is nothing worse than travelling down a road and not knowing where you're heading, because how will you know when you reach your destination? The PPL is a fantastic tool for mapping out your progress and ensuring that you don't miss your goals or head off in the wrong direction.

While the PPL is extremely powerful for mapping your journey, it's important to remember that everybody's destination will be different. Some investors might own five properties before they transition into the consolidation phase, while others might own 10-plus properties.

Age is another differentiating factor; your property-investment journey may start in your early 20s or it could begin in your 40s. This affects the age at which you will move between phases.

The PPL is broken down into three main phases (see figure 4.2):

- accumulation phase
- consolidation phase
- lifestyle phase.

Figure 4.2: Property portfolio lifecycle

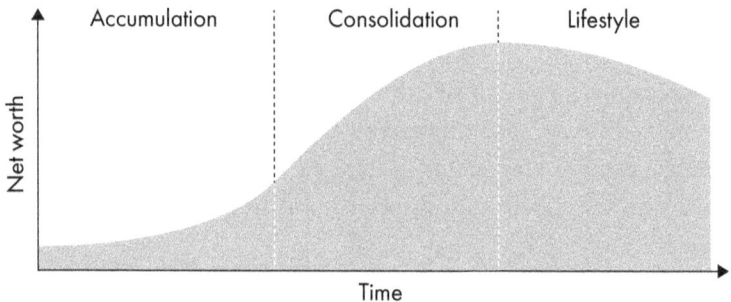

## Accumulation phase

For most investors, the accumulation phase is the most important stage of the investing journey, because this is when you build a strong and stable portfolio. The purpose of the accumulation phase is to acquire as many properties as you can. The properties should typically provide you with strong capital growth, which will enable you to continue scaling your portfolio.

The accumulation phase can be make or break for many investors. If you choose poor performing properties, not only will it take longer for you to move into the consolidation phase, but it may also substantially reduce your maximum portfolio potential. A poorly executed accumulation phase is the most common reason why less than 10 per cent of Australian property investors will ever own three or more properties.

## Consolidation phase

The next stage in the PPL is the consolidation phase. There is no definitive line in the sand that denotes when you will shift from the accumulation phase into the consolidation phase. Typically, this change will occur once you feel comfortable with the base of properties that you have acquired, and you may also begin looking at a higher quality of asset.

The consolidation phase is often typified by rapid and substantial growth in property value or cash flow on a year-on-year basis. It is also the stage when you are most likely to begin shifting from owning a large number of medium-quality properties to a smaller number of high-quality properties. What we often find is that as people move into the middle of their working life, the demands on their time become greater and they begin to look for ways to gain some of that time and effort back. An example of this is a mid to senior-level executive who may decide to reduce their portfolio from 10 properties down to five properties, ensuring that the five properties are high quality and often located in blue-chip suburbs. This will reduce the annual workload while ensuring that the port-folio still generates excellent returns despite the reduced number of overall assets being held.

This is also the period when you may begin to diversify your hold-ings from traditional residential real estate into other avenues such as commercial property. There can be multiple reasons for this shift, including greater awareness of risk and reward, a more confident understanding of how property and property investment operate and a forward outlook towards your needs during the lifestyle phase.

## Lifestyle phase

The lifestyle phase is all about being able to enjoy the spoils of your years of successful property investing. This final stage could hypo-thetically begin in your 30s or as late as your 60s and beyond.

The lifestyle phase occurs when your property portfolio can support your 'retirement' in whatever form you desire. For many investors, this will be a certain level of cash flow each year, while for others it will be a total portfolio value that they will slowly sell down to live off the proceeds. Every person will have a different benchmark, but each portfolio will be sufficient to meet this goal by the time it transitions into the lifestyle phase.

Before transitioning into the lifestyle phase, it is crucial to ensure that you have crunched the numbers on your cash flow and equity to ensure that your portfolio can support your desired lifestyle. The worst situation for any investor is to realise that your investments can't support you in the way that you intended them to, and you're forced to return to the workforce when you should be spending time with family and friends – not worrying about making ends meet.

## GEARING AND CASH FLOW

Gearing and cash flow are two very important aspects of property investment that are often misunderstood. It is quite common to hear people interchangeably refer to positive cash flow and positive gearing as the same thing, which is technically incorrect. When discussing these terms in relation to investments, gearing is used to talk about the return before tax, while cash flow is related to the after-tax position. In practical terms, an investor may have a negatively geared property that becomes cash flow positive after tax. This type of shift often occurs as a result of depreciation benefits that may be available for a particular investment, or from significantly higher mortgage interest payments compared to the level of rental income that is received.

There is no greater debate between property investors than whether you should invest based on a negative or positive gearing portfolio strategy. The debate is primarily based on the idea that blue-chip properties – those located in the inner or inner-middle ring of capital cities – are a better investment. These types of properties will often attract wealthier people with larger incomes, and it has been debated that because these properties are close to amenities and employment (like a CBD), they will grow quicker than properties in other locations. Due to their significant prices, most attract rental yields in the 2 to 3 per cent range, which leaves the owner unable to cover all expenses from the rental income; hence the property is negatively geared. Investors who believe in a negative gearing strategy choose this approach because they believe that the capital growth of the property will far exceed the potential cash loss each year, leaving them in a better overall position. This type of investor has typically been known as a capital growth investor.

On the opposite side of the coin are those investors who may be considered cash flow investors. The cash flow investor will invest in properties generate a yield of 7 or 8 per cent plus, hoping to purchase multiple properties and eventually replace their own salary with the rent from their properties. This type of strategy has usually required investors to invest in regional or high-risk remote areas that rely on cyclical employment industries such as mining. This type of investor was usually unconcerned with capital growth because their primary aim is to accumulate multiple high-cash-flow properties to replace their salary.

These two opposing types of investors were most prevalent during the late 1990s to late 2000s when lending was far more liberal, and investors could borrow a seemingly 'infinite' amount of money. This situation began to shift after the GFC and into the 2010s, when lenders and government regulatory bodies cracked down on lending standards and the previously 'infinite' lending tap was turned off.

Many well-known Australian property investors were able to ride this wave of loose lending standards during the 1990s and early 2000s, building themselves substantial property portfolios that consisted entirely of blue-chip homes. These properties were often located in highly sought-after locations like the eastern suburbs of Sydney and were highly negatively geared. Due to the lax lending, these investors were able to ride the significant growth these areas enjoyed, resulting in portfolios worth millions of dollars, and often comprising 10-plus properties. What a time that was to invest!

Unfortunately, for those people looking to begin or continue their journey in property investment today, it is not possible to replicate these portfolios of the past. We wish that it was, we truly do – if it were, we would be the first people to jump onboard. Thanks to the changes in lending standards, people just don't have the same ability to borrow and then keep borrowing.

In order to build a substantial property portfolio that is scalable and continues to enable you to keep purchasing every few years, you need to take on a hybrid approach of both strategies – if not leaning more towards the cash flow style.

You might be wondering what we mean by a substantial and scalable portfolio. To us, a substantial and scalable portfolio is a portfolio that consists of more than four properties and allows you to continue borrowing and purchasing property every few years. Today, by taking on a negative gearing approach, most investors will have their lending capped out after one property, or, if they're lucky, two. The investor would likely have to wait years and years before they would be able to purchase another property, and their overall financial freedom may take many years longer than they expected.

## PORTFOLIO END STATE

Your portfolio end state will be dictated by what you set as your overarching goal for investing. For some people, it will be to replace their salary with passive income from their portfolio so that they can spend more time with their family. Other people may decide that they want to build a large portfolio so that they can pass on generational wealth to their children and grandchildren. Whatever your reason for investing, your portfolio end state needs to reflect this. The two most common portfolio end states include a portfolio with substantial equity or a portfolio that provides passive income.

## Equity portfolio

The equity portfolio has been utilised by generations of people around the world. The equity portfolio is based off the idea of accumulating as many properties as possible; over time, the portfolio will provide a substantial increase in net worth. The equity portfolio is also the basis of most buy-and-hold portfolios from a strategy perspective and is the most common portfolio end state of blue-chip investors.

The equity portfolio relies on purchasing property that will experience substantial capital gains over the life of ownership of the asset. After this growth, the investor can then slowly sell properties during the lifestyle phase of the PPL to fund their eventual retirement. At the start of the chapter, we highlighted the growth of all capital cities over the last 30 years – considering the worst-performing capital city was Darwin with 417 per cent, we would still consider this as a capital growth approach, and you would've had a great result.

Table 4.2 is a simple example of an equity portfolio.

*Table 4.2: Example equity portfolio*

| Property | Purchase price | Rental yield | Annual growth | Value (in 30 years) |
|---|---|---|---|---|
| Property #1 | $800,000 | 3.0% | 7.5% | $7,003,964 |
| Property #2 | $700,000 | 3.5% | 7.0% | $5,328,578 |
| Property #3 | $850,000 | 2.8% | 8.0% | $8,553,258 |
| Property #4 | $680,000 | 3.6% | 7.0% | $5,176,333 |
| Portfolio value | $3,030,000 | | | $26,062,133 |

While we're sure that some of you will be sitting back and thinking, 'Well in that case, I'll just buy a few properties in Sydney and wait 30 years,' unfortunately that isn't the solution.

While the equity portfolio is fantastic, it is quite difficult to implement today. Over the last 10 years, there have been significant changes to lending conditions resulting in a reduced capacity to borrow money. This means that the average investor who takes the approach of purchasing a few properties in Sydney or Melbourne will have their lending capped out very quickly. Purchases in these cities are most likely to be highly negatively geared, meaning investors will have to pay from their own pocket each month to cover the mortgage repayments and other bills. The changes in lending we just spoke about mean that lenders will view your cash flow position quite negatively if you're in this situation, and the result will be a reduced lending capacity and a likelihood of only being able to purchase one to two properties.

**Passive income portfolio**

The passive income portfolio is designed to replace your regular salary and allow you to live life on your own terms while being 'paid' by your portfolio. Ultimately, you need money to survive, and the passive income portfolio enables this – while also allowing you to keep your portfolio. Unlike the equity strategy, there is no requirement to sell your properties every few years, which is an attractive idea to most people – particularly those who wish to pass on assets to children. The passive income portfolio can be achieved through residential property, commercial property or a combination of the two.

There is no question that commercial property provides superior cash flow compared with residential property, but commercial property also requires different knowledge and skills. While some property investors may purchase commercial property, the passive income portfolio is still achievable using residential property alone.

Now, this book does not dive into the specifics of commercial property; however, we would certainly recommend you learn more about this topic and incorporate commercial assets into your portfolio at the right time.

There are two common ways of building an income portfolio through residential property. The first is purchasing low-growth, high-cash-flow properties (otherwise known as cash cows – we'll look at these in Step 5 – Excellence) and then utilising the excess cash flow to build your passive income. The second method, which can be harder to forecast, is to purchase well-located properties and pay down the mortgages until the rental income becomes pure cash flow. While this method is preferable as you can also reap the benefit of capital growth, it is harder to forecast. A property in this portfolio type will ideally be slightly positively geared or neutrally geared at purchase, and you will be relying on future rental growth and an ability to pay down the mortgage before you can reap the benefits of passive income.

Let's take a look at a simple example of a passive income portfolio (table 4.3).

Table 4.3: Example passive income portfolio

| Property | Purchase price | Weekly rent | Rental yield | Annual expenses | Passive income (annual) |
|---|---|---|---|---|---|
| Property #1 | $200,000 | $370 | 9.62% | $6,940 | $12,300 |
| Property #2 | $220,000 | $390 | 9.21% | $7,563 | $12,717 |
| Property #3 | $220,000 | $390 | 9.21% | $7,563 | $12,717 |
| Property #4 | $250,000 | $400 | 8.32% | $8,414 | $12,386 |
| | | | | | $50,120 |

As you can see above, it is possible to accumulate over $50,000 of annual passive income by owning only four cash cow properties.

While the passive income looks great, don't forget that these properties are often located in less-desirable areas, may be prone to high vacancy rates and frequently have lower-quality tenants – nothing is perfect!

### Can you combine equity and passive income?

You've now read about equity portfolios and passive income portfolios, and we're sure you have started thinking about the type of portfolio you should build. We are asked by our clients every single week, 'Can we combine an equity and income portfolio?' The answer is an overwhelming *yes!* In fact, a combined approach is our suggestion for the typical person trying to invest in property and grow their wealth.

If you began your portfolio journey in the late 1990s or early 2000s you would've had much more favourable conditions to build a purely equity-based portfolio. If you decided to take a passive-income-only approach, you would have missed out on the generational wealth that can be created through equity. Based on the lending conditions of today, we believe that investors can find a middle ground between equity and passive income in their portfolios.

From our perspective, after building property portfolios for clients and ourselves, investors can achieve fantastic results through a careful balance of capital growth and cash flow (see figure 4.3). This balance is important because if you swing too much towards capital growth, you can risk limiting your ability to purchase future property; but if you move too close to cash flow, you risk losing massive capital gains and equity for future property deposits. The fine balance is very important in the investing environment of today, and this is where professional help can be beneficial.

We think that a balanced portfolio starts with solid cash flow. When purchasing a property, if you can ensure that the rental yield is at least 4.5 per cent, this will promote strong cash flow to ensure you can keep borrowing for future properties. Capital growth is tricky because nobody has a crystal ball that can tell us what the growth of a property will be. In the next chapter we will take you through some of the contributing factors; however, the main thing to remember is that you want to try to purchase property that is at the start of its growth cycle. In Step 5 – Excellence, we will show you how powerful it is to purchase property at the start of the growth cycle, and being able to reap those rewards at the start instead of waiting for the property to grow at the end of the cycle. The fantastic part of this approach is that properties that fit these requirements are often located in some of the smaller capital cities or major regional centres with populations that rival some cities. This is a bonus because these markets suffer fewer issues around housing affordability and they can possess great fundamentals for long-term growth.

### Figure 4.3: Optimal portfolio

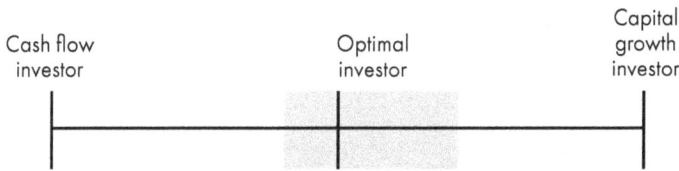

Cash flow investor       Optimal investor       Capital growth investor

Table 4.4 highlights a great example of the start of a combined portfolio. This type of portfolio can usually be purchased within a few years and can provide a small passive income while not sacrificing future capital growth. This type of portfolio would also be well received by a lender for future loans as the properties are able to pay for themselves, leaving any excess income available for future property loans.

While the example in the equity strategy looked great on paper, it is not achievable by most investors today. The investor holding the equity portfolio is likely to have been capped out of future lending by property number two, and the investor would not have been able to borrow for many more years – significantly reducing their portfolio growth. While the equity portfolio may be achievable by high-earning investors, this is not the scenario for most everyday people looking to build a portfolio.

The combined equity and passive income portfolio, however, is an achievable portfolio structure for the typical investor. It allows you to build a portfolio that will assist in funding your retirement while also ensuring capital growth for generational wealth or additional comfort in retirement.

*Table 4.4: Example combined portfolio*

| Property | Purchase price | Weekly rent | Passive income (annual) | Annual growth | Value (30 years) |
|---|---|---|---|---|---|
| Property #1 | $400,000 | $400 | $7,000 | 5.0% | $1,728,776 |
| Property #2 | $380,000 | $390 | $7,350 | 5.5% | $1,893,901 |
| Property #3 | $450,000 | $425 | $6,800 | 6.0% | $2,584,571 |
| Property #4 | $510,000 | $450 | $7,150 | 5.0% | $2,204,190 |
| Portfolio value | $1,740,000 | $1,665 | $28,300 | | $8,411,438 |

Knowledge is the bedrock of professional mastery. This chapter has been about ensuring that you have a great understanding of property-investment basics and how they work together for you to achieve financial freedom. As a savvy and wise property investor, you will know where you sit within your PPL and what types of property portfolio strategies you need to be employing to move into your next stage. By combining your understanding of what type of portfolio you would like to create and where you are in your portfolio lifecycle, you will have a huge leg up on your competition in the property market.

# Step 5:
# EXCELLENCE

When a military professional strives for professional mastery, they know that it can never truly be attained. What can be achieved in place of professional mastery is excellence. Excellence is the by-product of discipline and dedication to mastering your profession. It is excellence that drives the military professional to be better than their enemy and it is excellence that allows them to seamlessly execute and achieve their mission, no matter the challenge that is posed.

Step 1: Reveille

Step 2: Discipline

Step 3: Teamwork

Step 4: Professional mastery

**Step 5: Excellence**

Step 6: Mission analysis

Step 7: Courage

Step 8: Adaptability and flexibility

Step 9: Dedication

Step 10: Loyalty

## Step 5: Excellence

Excellence in property investing does not come easily. By now we're sure that you've realised how much there is to learn about property and how tricky it can be to get right. To achieve excellence in property investing, it is so important to continue learning and practising your skills until you are able to seamlessly execute them. With that in mind, this step is about teaching you the knowledge you will need to achieve excellence when you are investing in property.

### DWELLING TYPES

Much like how the share market has different types of companies that you can invest in (technology, banks, resources and so on), the property market also has different types of assets that you can invest in.

The property market can be separated into two different overarching types of assets: residential and commercial.

Residential property is what most investors typically think about when they consider investing in real estate. There are many different types of residential properties (which we will break down shortly) but they all have a common feature – their primary purpose is for somebody to live in them. In Australia, at time of writing, the residential property market is worth over $8.4 trillion and there are over 10.6 million dwellings, whereas the total value of the ASX is between $2.5 trillion and $3 trillion. To put this into context, residential real estate is by far the largest single type of asset by value in Australia.

Commercial property, on the other hand, is exactly as the name suggests – commercial! The primary purpose of commercial properties is for a business to utilise the asset for its business needs. These needs can vary, from retail shopfronts like supermarkets, office spaces for businesses and warehouses for industrial companies.

Table 5.1 lists some of the different types of residential and commercial properties.

*Table 5.1: Types of residential and commercial properties*

| Residential | Commercial |
|---|---|
| House | Retail |
| Land | Office |
| Apartment | Industrial |
| Townhouse | |
| Duplex | |
| Granny flat | |

## Houses

The first type of residential dwelling we're going to cover, and the most common, is houses. Houses are best characterised as single buildings on a plot of land where the owner controls both the building and the land. Houses can be multistorey, and typical block sizes in capital cities range from 300 m² all the way up to 1,200 m². Houses come in a range of styles. In Australia, we have the classic Queenslander: a single-storey weatherboard home, elevated off the ground to promote airflow in hot and humid environments. Federation-style homes are commonly found around Melbourne: these are often small brick or weatherboard homes with dark colours, small verandahs and decorative windows. Today, houses have shifted to a 'modern' style, characterised by the use of glass, marble, stone, sharp edges and rendered facades.

In general, houses are an excellent investment. Since the value of a property is in the land, as the building depreciates over time, investors should try to own as much land as possible. By owning and controlling the land, you have substantially more choice available as to what you would like to do with the property. There are considerably less restrictions on the activities you can undertake if you own and control the land – from developing the land into multiple dwellings, to other activities such as a knockdown and rebuild. If you owned another dwelling type, say an apartment, you would only control a very small portion of land. As an owner, you aren't free to develop or improve the apartment at your leisure because the owner's corporation often has to approve works, and the majority of your asset (the apartment itself) is going to depreciate over time.

## Land

Our second type of residential asset to discuss is land. Land is exactly what you think it is – a patch of dirt that might have some grass, and is waiting for a building to be built on top of it. Land is so important because it is what gives a property its enduring value. Homes can always be built, demolished and rebuilt on the same piece of land, but there will never be an 'extra' piece of land. Land is finite, particularly in desirable areas like major cities. Since land is limited, the law of supply and demand is what enables our properties to keep gaining value, even when the building may have been constructed way back in the 1950s!

Supply and demand is also the reason why waterfront properties are so expensive – the coastline and its underlying land simply can't be increased, so demand for these properties will always be significantly higher than the available supply, which results in big upswings in prices over time.

## Apartments

Our third dwelling type to discuss is apartments. Apartments can be thought of as small pieces of an overall building. The building could be as small as two or three levels, or it could be a large skyscraper and have over 40 floors! The appeal of apartments has grown in recent years, most notably due to the ever-increasing issue of house affordability. If you then add in more working professionals who desire to be close to the city where they work and socialise, you can see why the appeal of apartments has rapidly grown over the last few decades.

While apartments have a number of appealing features from an owner-occupier perspective, they can have a number of downsides if you are looking at them for investment. First and foremost, apartments have very small pieces of land attached to them. Since apartment buildings are primarily built upwards and not sideways, all apartment owners have to share the small piece of land that the overall building sits on. This proposition might not be as bad if you purchase in a building with five or six apartments, but if you purchase an apartment in a building with 100 apartments, your slice of the land pie becomes awfully small.

The next big downside is that apartment buildings are controlled by a body corporate, owners corporation or strata scheme. These entities typically represent all the apartment owners in the building. The state you live in will often dictate which title is used, but the overarching role is to effectively govern a building that has multiple owners. Not only do apartments come with additional levies that can be thousands of dollars per quarter, but they are required to abide by strict rules set by their committees regarding what can and can't be done within the complex.

Imagine being told that you can't install pay TV, or that you can't carry out planned renovations to make your apartment more appealing for a buyer. This is the reality that most apartment owners will face during their ownership of an apartment. From an investing perspective, the limited land attached to an apartment, significant additional fees/levies and the inability to modify your property as you desire are all extremely concerning for the overall growth of your asset and portfolio.

### Townhouses

Our next residential dwelling type is townhouses. Townhouses are almost like a cross between an apartment and a house. Townhouses will most often be multistorey buildings that are bigger than apartments but don't have the land size or backyards that a typical house would have. Townhouses have become increasingly popular in inner-ring suburbs that don't have the space for houses but have the demand for properties that are bigger than apartments. Depending on the construction, townhouses may be part of a body corporate, owners corporation or strata scheme, or they may be standalone properties. In Canberra, you'll find many townhouses are part of an overall body corporate organisation, while most townhouses in the inner west of Sydney are standalone properties.

From an investment point of view, townhouses can either be excellent or low-performing. As we have discussed, the primary value of a property is in the land – and, unfortunately for most townhouse owners, their land is still very limited. The upside of townhouses is that they can be located in very desirable areas that may not have houses, so they are the next-best alternative to an apartment. Another advantage of townhouses that are not part of body corporate, owner's corporation or strata schemes is that you can usually develop or renovate them exactly how you would a house. This could provide an investor many different opportunities to increase the value of their property that would not ordinarily be available to them if they owned an apartment. All in all, townhouses can make very good investments if they are analysed correctly, and can provide you opportunity to add value through development and/or renovation at a later date.

### Duplexes

Our penultimate dwelling type is the duplex. A duplex is a larger-than-normal house that has been divided down the middle to create two separate houses. The two separate houses will then be lived in by separate people who will often have their own driveway and backyard – almost like a normal house! A duplex can be on a single title, or it can be separated into two separate titles – almost like giving owners two properties for the price of one. A duplex can make a great investment for the astute investor. Since a duplex can have two separate tenants, it is possible for the property to have a gross yield of 7 to 8 per cent, which is noticeably higher than a well-located house that may have a 4 to 5 per cent gross yield. Another advantage of a duplex is that if the property is on a single title, there may be the potential to split it into two separate titles, effectively creating a second property and substantially increasing equity in your portfolio.

While there are plenty of benefits, duplexes can have some negatives. The biggest downside is that they are often located in large estates where there is a massive amount of housing supply, which will affect the future capital growth of the property. It is very rare to be able to find a duplex (or build a duplex) in an established neighbourhood where supply has already been extinguished. The second downside is that a duplex can have a body corporate, owners corporation or strata scheme because there is common property. For a duplex, the common property can be as little as a shared driveway or letterbox area, but this common property may bring the unwanted fees and levies that would more commonly be expected with an apartment.

### Granny flats

Our final dwelling type is the granny flat. A granny flat is a small building that is constructed in the backyard of an existing house and is then tenanted out separately to the main dwelling. Granny flats can be an extremely cost-effective method of increasing a property's weekly cash flow, thereby increasing your borrowing capacity and/or reducing your loan commitments. Granny flats are usually tightly regulated by the local council and this can sometimes result in the construction of unapproved granny flats on properties (be careful!). Although a granny flat can bring substantial cash flow into your portfolio, you need to remain aware that the pool of people who may buy your property in the future may become much more limited. If you have a well-located house in a great suburb and then build a granny flat, a potential owner-occupier may not be as inclined to purchase your property if they don't have a need for a separate dwelling. This means that your pool of potential purchasers is reduced to only investors, and investors are far more likely to drive a hard bargain during the negotiation process.

## Commercial property

As the name suggests, commercial property is property that exists for a commercial purpose. Commercial property is typically separated into three categories: retail, office and industrial. Over the years, there has been a rise in alternative-type commercial properties (which often do fit into one of these three categories); examples include childcare, storage and data centres.

The predominant difference between residential and commercial property is that commercial property is valued based on the lease. In layperson's terms, this means that if two identical properties existed and one had a one-year lease and the other had a five-year lease, the property with the five-year lease would be perceived to have a higher value. Table 5.2 takes a quick dive into the different types of commercial property.

*Table 5.2: Types of commercial property*

| Property type | Description |
| --- | --- |
| Retail properties | Properties that primarily sell goods to a customer from the building. Some common examples of retail properties are clothing stores and electronics stores. |
| Office properties | Properties that primarily function as office space for businesses. These types of properties can range from CBD skyscrapers with multiple floors through to single-storey offices in the suburbs. While the size of the properties can vary significantly, the most common category of business to utilise this type of property will be professional services such as lawyers and accountants, or corporate headquarters. |
| Industrial properties | Properties that are primarily used for industrial purposes. Industrial purposes can include activities such as storage, logistics and manufacturing. |

## BUYING NEW VERSUS ESTABLISHED RESIDENTIAL PROPERTY

It's now time to give our perspective on one of the greatest debates in residential property investment – which provides superior investment potential: new or established property?

Throughout this book, you will see that we have a very strong bias towards established property. In a couple of moments, we will take you through the reasons why, but above all else, established property has worked well for our portfolio and those of our clients. Some people have done well with portfolios based on purchasing new property, but we would argue that in general terms, established will always outperform new.

### Supply and demand

One of the biggest reasons we believe in established properties over new properties is supply and demand. While there are lots of factors that underpin property price growth, fundamentally, supply and demand is what it all boils down to. Unfortunately for new property, the supply side of the equation is disastrously out of balance. Most new properties are built in large property estates, where most of the other properties are new as well. As sales rise, developers will continuously list more and more plots of land for sale. This means that developers control the supply of properties in the market. If there is no demand, developers just don't list properties for sale. When demand begins to rise, developers continue to release properties until the demand has been satisfied. This means that it is very difficult for natural market pressure, which drives up property prices, to occur – it is all in the hands of the developer.

### Location

Our next reason is location. Major cities have already been built out from the centre, and there are generally no opportunities close to the centre for developers to purchase large parcels of land to then develop into estates. Developers are required to purchase their large parcels of land on the outer fringes of cities, because that is the only place where this volume of land is now available. This means that those living in these outer-fringe suburbs are far away from CBDs, quality schools, renowned shopping areas and transport hubs – would you want to live in a place so dislocated?

## Depreciation

There are several mathematical reasons to choose established over new properties. Let's start with depreciation. Developers of new properties will continuously push the benefits of depreciation upon interested buyers. However, as an investor, you know that you should be looking to purchase a high-value, appreciating *asset*, not a depreciating *liability*. Although tax depreciations may seem attractive (and your tax return may put a few extra thousand dollars back in your pocket), property investors want to spend as little money as possible on a depreciating asset.

For both new and established properties, it is paramount to remember that the value of the asset is in the land – not in the build. Let's look at an example, illustrated in tables 5.3 and 5.4.

*Table 5.3: Value – example established property*

| Total value of the property | $600,000 |
|---|---|
| Land value | $375,000 |
| House value | $225,000 |

*Table 5.4: Value – example new property*

| Total value of the property | $600,000 |
|---|---|
| Land value | $225,000 |
| House value | $375,000 |

Both properties are the same value, however the new property will have the 'depreciation benefits', as marketed by the developer, attached to the new $375,000 house. What buyers don't see is that they are purchasing a property that has a reduced land value ($225,000) when compared to the asset of the existing property ($375,000).

Always remember: the value is in the land. This is why house and land packages are sold on significantly smaller pieces of land than established properties – with tiny front and back yards. Developers know that the value is in the land, so they attempt to divide it up as much as possible in order to put more dwellings on it and sell to more buyers who are captivated by the beautiful, brand-new property and the glossy brochures. When buyers inspect new properties in freshly established estates, they are too busy looking at the huge amount of 'house' they are getting for their money, rather than being concerned with the lack of land in the front, back and side yards.

Let's look at our example again (tables 5.5 and 5.6).

*Table 5.5: Value and result – example established property*

| Total value of the property | $600,000 | Result |
|---|---|---|
| Land value | $375,000 | More of your money is going to the asset |
| House value | $225,000 | Less of your money is going to the liability |

*Table 5.6: Value and result – example new property*

| Total value of the property | $600,000 | Result |
|---|---|---|
| Land value | $225,000 | Less of your money is going to the asset |
| House value | $375,000 | More of your money is going to the liability (spruiked as 'depreciation benefits') |

If you buy a new property, more of your money is purchasing a liability rather than an asset that will grow over time and provide you with scalable capital gains.

Another point to note is that whenever you purchase a new house and land package, there will always be a developer's fee hidden within the purchase price. Buyers of new properties need to be aware that they will rarely pay fair market price for a new build. Developers have to earn their money from somewhere, right?

### Capital gains

Now, let's use our example to look at the appreciation of the two different properties. Let's analyse the example after 10 years of growth, during which time we'll assume that the properties' value will have doubled, and that the buildings will have depreciated at the same rate of 15 per cent each (see tables 5.7 and 5.8).

*Table 5.7: Value after 10 years – example established property*

| Land value | $750,000 | Asset |
| House value | $191,250 | Liability |
| **Total value** | **$941,250** | **An increase of $341,250** |

*Table 5.8: Value after 10 years – example new property*

| Land value | $450,000 | Asset |
| House value | $318,750 | Liability |
| **Total value** | **$768,750** | **An increase of $168,750** |

The difference in the appreciated value of the two properties is *$172,500*.

As you can see, after appreciating the land and depreciating the property, the established property is in a league of its own, while the new property has fallen behind in value. This illustrates the importance of land value and ensuring that your future property investments have enough of it.

### Tax benefits

Now, let's tackle the 'tax benefit' argument for new properties. Developers and other investors who choose new properties over established will often say, 'Just think about all of the tax benefits for the new property! Established-property buyers certainly don't reap those benefits.'

This is correct – if you count spending money as a 'benefit'. Remember, as an investor you want to see your asset appreciating while pocketing as much cash as possible, not spending it or seeing it diminish over time. As you can see in the previous examples, the land of the established property is appreciating at a rate that a new property's 'tax benefits' could simply never keep up with. We would be surprised if any investor could claim $172,500 worth of tax depreciation, even at the highest marginal tax rate of 45 per cent.

Again, the value in property is in the capital gains, not in the alleged 'tax savings'.

As you can see, established property will mathematically outperform new properties and this is why we personally choose to bolster our portfolios with high-performing, established properties.

## PROPERTY FINANCE

Property investing is a game of finance. This phrase has been said by countless property investors, regardless of experience, because every investor has been faced with the realities of being unable to borrow funds. The reason why property is a game of finance is because without being able to borrow money, most investors will not be able to purchase properties. The game begins when you use all of your borrowing capacity with one lender, and you commence the cat-and-mouse game of trying to find different lenders that are willing to lend you money.

Before we get into the intricacies of property finance, let's quickly explain what a loan is and then expand on the different types of loans that you would typically see on offer in Australia.

A loan is comprised of two parts: principal and interest. The principal is the amount of money that you borrow, and the interest is what the bank will charge you as a fee for using their money.

Let's look at a quick example. Charlotte decides to borrow $100,000 from her bank at a rate of 5 per cent interest per annum. Each year, at 5 per cent, Charlotte will be charged $5,000 of interest.

In this example, the $100,000 that Charlotte borrowed is the *principal* and the $5,000 is the *interest*.

In Australia, there are typically two types of loans and two ways that interest is applied to the loan. The two types of loans are principal and interest, and interest only, and the two methods of interest are fixed and variable (see table 5.9).

*Table 5.9: Types of loans and interest*

| Types of loans | Types of interest |
| --- | --- |
| Principal and interest | Fixed |
| Interest only | Variable |

With a principal-and-interest loan, where you make a set repayment each month and that repayment covers the interest and a portion of the principal. The loan is typically paid down over 30 years and results in a paid-off mortgage at the end of the period. On the other hand, an interest-only loan only pays off the interest each month, as opposed to also paying a portion of the principal. The end result of an interest-only loan is that the principal is still remaining at the end of the loan term.

So why would anybody choose an interest-only loan where you never pay down your mortgage? The first reason, and the most common, is cash flow. As you will see in our example below (table 5.10), a principal-and-interest loan that has the same interest rate as an interest-only loan will always have a higher monthly repayment. If you're a property investor, it is usually accepted that you want to retain as much cash as possible because cash is what may be the deposit on your next property. By choosing an interest-only loan, you may be better off by hundreds of additional dollars each month, which could be saved for your next deposit.

*Table 5.10: Repayment breakdown – principal and interest versus interest only*

| Principal-and-interest loan | | Interest-only loan | |
|---|---|---|---|
| Principal: | $100,000 | Principal: | $100,000 |
| Interest rate: | 5% | Interest rate: | 5% |
| Monthly repayment: | $536.82 | Monthly repayment: | $416.67 |
| Repayment difference: | +$120.15 | Repayment difference: | -$120.15 |

The second reason that investors typically utilise interest-only loans is for tax deduction purposes. For most (if not all) investors, the interest on a mortgage is tax deductible for an investment property. Unfortunately, the principal component is not a tax deduction. Since investors can claim the entire mortgage payment on tax, and the repayments are lower than principal and interest loans, it is not hard to see why investors are more likely to choose an interest-only loan.

Let's take a quick look at the two different types of interest – fixed and variable. A fixed interest rate is exactly what it sounds like: it's fixed. This means that, despite what may happen to other loan products that the lender offers, your fixed interest rate will not change. Most fixed interest rate products will have a fixed period of between one and five years. After this time, the loan will become variable, and it is quite common for the variable rate to be higher than what is being advertised as a variable rate to the general public. Many investors will simply refinance their existing fixed rate loan product into a new fixed rate loan product when their initial fixed period expires. This means that you could hypothetically remain on a fixed rate for your whole period of ownership of the property. Practically, many investors will eventually switch to a variable loan at some point in the future because a variable loan can be easier to pay out if you ever sell the property.

Just like a fixed rate loan, a variable rate is exactly what it sounds like – its variable! A variable rate loan will have a varying interest rate, depending on the interest rate the bank decides to set. Now, banks don't just change the interest rates for no reason – rate changes will usually be linked to changes in the overall economic situation in Australia. Some common reasons for changes in loan interest rates are when the Reserve Bank of Australia (RBA) changes the official cash rate, or if the government announces a major uplift or downturn in the overall economy.

Some lenders will also allow borrowers to make their loan partially fixed and partially variable – known as a split home loan. For example, you might take out a $500,000 loan and decide to split it with $300,000 on a fixed rate and $200,000 on a variable rate. This can be a powerful option if you would like to have some certainty around loan repayments, but you would also like to take advantage of future changes in interest rates.

So, should you choose a fixed or variable mortgage? Well, the answer is that either can be the right choice. If you think that interest rates are going to rise, you might choose to fix your mortgage. This will then mean that when others are paying higher rates, you are still fixed at the lower rate. If the opposite is true and you believe interest rates will go down, you would probably look to take on a variable rate loan. In this situation, those people who chose to fix their mortgage will be stuck with higher repayments, while those on a variable loan will see their repayments lower.

The other common consideration for investors is cash flow planning. Regardless of interest rates, a fixed mortgage will give you surety around what your monthly repayments will be. This means that you can plan your cash flow well in advance, and this could be a pivotal point in the decision of whether or not to invest. If you choose a variable mortgage, cash flow can be harder to project because your interest rate may go up or down, and in turn your repayments will also go up or down. The most common mortgage combinations (not including split loans) are:

- principal and interest (fixed)
- principal and interest (variable)
- interest only (fixed)
- interest only (variable).

Now that we know all about the different types of loans, let's have a chat about the different types of lenders. In Australia, the different lenders are usually separated into 'tiers'. At the top, we have tier 1 lenders. Tier 1 lenders are usually considered to be the Big 4 banks. The idea of the Big 4 being tier 1 is due to them writing the vast majority of loans within Australia, so they comprise the top level of lenders.

Now, the following tiers can often result in some debate, but here is our perspective on it. At the next level down, tier 2, we have all the other banks that aren't the Big 4. Some of these banks are actually owned by one of the Big 4, so you are still part of the wider ecosystem of the tier 1 banks.

Then we arrive at the tier 3 lenders. Tier 3 comprises every other organisation that is willing to loan people money for the purposes of a mortgage. Most of the tier 3 lenders are businesses that are not banks, and this means that they can have very different standards to what you may be used to.

It's important to understand that there are different types of lenders because property is a game of finance, right? Each of the different lenders will have its own criteria for assessing borrowing capacity and loans. In very generic terms, tier 1 lenders are more likely to assess your borrowing capacity on a stricter basis than tier 2 lenders, and the same for tier 2 compared with tier 3. This is important to understand because the order in which you receive finance from different lenders is crucial. The aim should be for you to utilise your full borrowing capacity from the strictest lender first, and then work back in order from strictest to easiest. The reason for this is because if you utilise your borrowing capacity from the easiest lender first, by the time you get to the strictest they will more than likely say that they will not lend you any more money. By going from strictest to easiest, you are likely to be in a better lending position towards the end – and this could be the difference between purchasing your next property or not!

Unfortunately, there is no magical order that is the same for everybody. One person may have one order of lenders, but another person may have a totally different order. This is where a mortgage broker is key! As we discussed in Step 3 – Teamwork, a mortgage broker will be very comfortable with a wide variety of lenders and is in the best position to advise you on the best order based on your personal circumstances. Befriend a great mortgage broker.

## THE POWER OF EQUITY

In property, equity is simply the difference between the value of the property and any outstanding loans against it. If you have a

$500,000 property with a $400,000 mortgage, you have $100,000 of equity. Equity is important because it is what you would receive if you sold the property, or it can be used for future property deposits.

There are two ways to gain more equity in a property:

1. You can pay down your mortgage.
2. The property can grow in value.

The first option is essentially a principal and interest loan, and the second option is when the market that your property sits within grows in value over time. For your property to grow, the market will be realising a shortage of supply relative to demand, and prospective buyers will be willing to pay more money to purchase your property.

Believe it or not, you can also help your property grow in value by making strategic improvements. One of the most common examples of this is a cosmetic renovation. This is where you make improvements to older areas of your property, such as the kitchen or bathroom, and improve them to a more modern standard. These enhanced features will make the property more appealing to the market and therefore increase your equity in the property. If you're a property investor, the aim of a cosmetic renovation is to achieve a greater equity return than the actual money you have invested. Most investors should aim to achieve between $2 and $3 of equity gain for every $1 invested in the renovation (see table 5.11).

*Table 5.11: Equity gain for a cosmetic renovation*

| | |
|---|---|
| Property value before renovation: | $500,000 |
| Kitchen renovation cost: | $20,000 |
| Property value after renovation: | $560,000 |
| Equity uplift: | $60,000 |
| Return on investment: | $2 for every $1 spent, or 200% |

Now, we can hear many of you asking the same question that we get asked daily: 'So, what is the power of equity, other than it being the money we would receive if we sold?' Well, equity is the secret weapon to allow you to purchase your next investment property sooner!

As your property naturally grows in the market, so too does your equity. Now, banks and lenders actually recognise that your property can grow in value and that this could accumulate into a substantial amount of wealth that is just sitting there. As we touched on in Step 2 – Discipline, lenders will allow you to borrow against the potential equity in your property, if your loan to value ratio (LVR) is low enough. Typically, lenders prefer you to have a LVR of below 80 per cent, and they then let you borrow 80 per cent of the amount below that (see table 5.12).

*Table 5.12: Useable equity example*

| Property value: | $600,000 |
|---|---|
| Mortgage: | $400,000 |
| Loan to value ratio: | 66% |
| Useable equity: | 80% - 66% = 14% |
| Useable equity value: | 14% × 80% × $600,000 = $67,200 |

As you can see in table 5.12, the property has useable equity of $67,200, which is a substantial amount of money and more than enough to fund the deposit and closing costs for another investment property.

The power of equity is great, but we actually skipped a step! We didn't explain what underpins the power of equity and how it works. The power of equity is a fancy way of describing compound growth. Compound growth occurs when you earn growth on the growth you earned in a previous period. If you had $100 and you earned 10 per cent interest per annum, you would end up with $110 by the end of the year. The fantastic thing about compounding is that in the next year, you would earn your 10 per cent interest off $110 and not the original $100 – resulting in $121 – an extra $1 of interest compared to the year before. Let's apply this in a property scenario (table 5.13).

*Table 5.13: Compound growth example – single property*

|  | Year 1 | Year 2 |
|---|---|---|
| Property value | $400,000 | $428,000 |
| Annual growth rate | 7% | 7% |
| Annual growth | $28,000 | $29,960 |
| New property value | $428,000 | $457,960 |

In year 1, the property grew by $28,000, then in year 2, the property grew by $29,960 – an extra $1,960! This extra growth is an example of compounding in action. Although this was only a small gain, let's take a quick look at how compounding can affect an entire portfolio (table 5.14).

*Table 5.14: Compound growth example – entire portfolio*

|  | Year 1 | Year 2 |
|---|---|---|
| Portfolio value | $6,500,000 | $6,955,000 |
| Annual growth rate | 7% | 7% |
| Annual growth | $455,000 | $486,850 |
| New portfolio value | $6,955,000 | $7,441,850 |

While it can be hard to value the effect of compounding on small numbers, it's much easier to see the power when looking at an overall portfolio. In one year, our portfolio gained an extra $31,850!

## PROPERTY STRATEGIES

In the same way that a military operation can utilise a variety of strategies to achieve the mission's aim, a property investor also has multiple property strategies at their disposal. Where the military might use a strategy that combines land and sea assets, property investors can implement different property-specific strategies based on the level of involvement and effort they would like to put in. Generally, property investors can be classified as either active or passive investors, but there are also strategies where an investor can become a hybrid of both types – a semi-active investor. The outcome of each strategy can be broadly grouped into either capital growth or cash flow.

As investors transition through their portfolio lifecycle, most will find that they utilise combinations of property-investment strategies, particularly as goals and timelines change throughout their journey. For example, it is quite common for an investor who utilises a buy-and-hold strategy to eventually conduct a renovation on a property that has become outdated and undergone a reasonable amount of wear and tear over time.

Table 5.15 outlines a list of implementable strategies for everyday Australian property investors. We'll then examine each strategy in more detail.

*Table 5.15: Property portfolio strategies*

| Strategy | Outcome | Suitable investor type |
|---|---|---|
| Buy and hold | Capital growth | Passive investor |
| Renovation | Capital growth | Semi-active investor |
| Flipping | Capital growth | Active investor |
| Cash cow | Cash flow | Passive investor |
| Secondary dwelling | Cash flow | Semi-active investor |

| Strategy | Outcome | Suitable investor type |
|---|---|---|
| Development: <br> • Subdivision <br> • Splitting <br> • Knock down and rebuild <br> • Knock down and build (<$5 million) <br> • Knock down and build (>$5 million) | Capital growth | Active investor |

### Buy and hold

The buy-and-hold strategy is the most common approach utilised by property investors around Australia. The strategy is exactly what it sounds like – investors buy a property and then hold it over the long term. This type of strategy is targeted at those who are primarily seeking capital growth from their investment and wish to take a more hands-off or passive approach. The buy-and-hold strategy adopts a passive approach because it relies on the natural growth of the market to increase the value of the property, without the investor having to do anything other than owning the property.

To ensure that you give yourself the best chance of success with this strategy, you should be purchasing a property with the expectation that you will be holding it for at least 10 years. Since this is a passive strategy and relies on the natural market movements, a 10-year timeline means that you should experience at least one full property cycle – ideally translating into doubling the original value of the property.

One of the biggest pitfalls we see from investors is that they want to employ a buy-and-hold passive strategy, but they only hold onto the property for a couple of years. After a few years, the investor might feel that the property hasn't performed at the level they expected, and they choose to sell. After considering all the mortgage costs, acquisition costs and selling costs, the investor ends up with an overall loss and becomes disillusioned with the idea of investing in property. If the investor held the property for only a little bit of extra time, the property might have experienced the growth they desired and resulted in a great overall investment. Unfortunately, whether it was through impatience or unrealistic expectations, this type of investor has missed out on an amazing opportunity to grow their wealth.

This is a very common situation, and it often arises because people think that property grows at a linear rate – for example, 5 per cent year-on-year. Realistically, the property will grow at different rates each year but will average out to 5 per cent per annum. In a practical sense, this means that some years the property may grow at 9 to 12 per cent and in other years it may grow at 2 to 3 per cent. But over a rough 10-year period, the rate of growth averages out to 5 per cent.

In the example illustrated in figure 5.1, an investor purchases a property for $500,000 and holds it for 10 years. The property grows at an annualised rate of 6 per cent. As you can see, the property finishes the period with a value of just under $900,000, which is a great result from a passive strategy. Each line of the graph represents a different scenario in terms of the rate of growth at particular times during the holding period, however each averages out to 6 per cent annualised growth. The top line shows higher growth years occurring at the start of the holding period; the middle line illustrates a smooth, consistent growth rate of 6 per cent; while the bottom line shows lower growth at the start of the period.

Too many investors expect their property to grow at a consistent rate throughout their ownership. This assumption simply isn't practical. In the optimal example illustrated in figure 5.1, the property grows at a rate between 10 and 12 per cent for the first three years but then slows to a rate of 3 to 5 per cent for the final seven years. Then consider the suboptimal example: if the investor sold the property after year five, they would be $165,000 worse off than in the optimal scenario (not including costs), but if they continued to hold the property until the end of year 10 it would have the same value as the optimal growth rate example. While it certainly is not ideal to have the growth occur on the back end of the period, it's important to understand where a property is in its cycle and that you may still be able to achieve a good result by holding on to the property for longer.

Figure 5.1: Buy and hold example

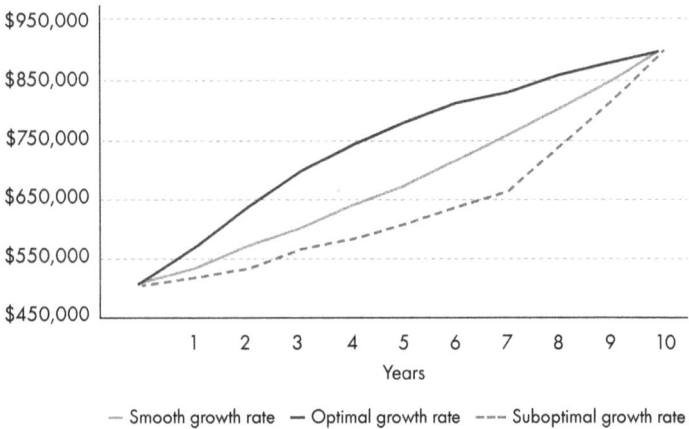

— Smooth growth rate   — Optimal growth rate   --- Suboptimal growth rate

**Renovation**

While the buy-and-hold strategy suits passive investors, the renovation strategy is for those people who are looking to be a little more active in their investment journey. If you are looking to employ a renovation strategy, you are still adhering to the idea of buying and holding the property – you're just adding in the concept of creating some value yourself. Where buy and hold relies only on natural market growth, the renovation strategy allows you to take some control of your investment's capital growth.

Renovation is not to be confused with flipping (which we will discuss next). Flipping takes a short-term outlook on the investment, whereas renovation still utilises the long-term-hold aspect of the buy-and-hold strategy.

Renovation is an extremely powerful tool for investors who are looking to generate value and growth, particularly in a market that may have stagnated (as all markets eventually do). Through renovations that can be as simple as fresh paint and new carpets, all the way up to brand-new kitchens, bathrooms or floorplans, property investors can manufacture their own capital growth when the market is not performing.

When considering renovating, it's helpful to look at higher-value surrounding properties to see where your property is inferior and what the most economical and advantageous improvements would be. This approach will also help to ensure you don't overcapitalise your renovations, which is where you spend more money than you receive in value.

### Flipping

For the active investor who is seeking a bigger and faster return than a traditional renovation, the option to 'flip' a property may be a good alternative. Unlike a typical renovation, where an investor may have held the property for several years or intends to keep the property for several years, flipping usually takes place over a few months.

Flipping involves purchasing a property solely for the purpose of renovating and then selling it once the renovation is complete. The idea behind the strategy is that an active investor can purchase a property that is in a cosmetic and/or structurally poor condition and then create value by repairing and enhancing the property. Some people might think of the strategy as 'finding a diamond in the rough' or improving 'the worst property in the best street.'

As mentioned previously, this strategy is certainly best suited to an active and experienced investor. To ensure a good investment return, it is crucial to purchase the property at the right price, and then fund and complete the renovations in a timely fashion to sell the property expeditiously. The two most obvious risks for an inexperienced investor are overpaying for the property and overcapitalising in the renovation. Since most flippers are seeking a return of at least 15 to 25 per cent, overpaying by even $5,000 can reduce the return quite substantially. Similarly, if you invest too much into the renovation and the market doesn't see the value in the improvements, you can also diminish your investment return.

While this strategy can be implemented quite successfully in Australia, it is more difficult than in other countries such as the United States (just think about all the American renovation shows). The main reason for this is that in Australia, you are required to pay stamp duty, which can add tens of thousands of dollars to your purchase. In other places, like the United States, stamp duty is replaced by an annual tax which substantially reduces the cost of entry but can raise the total cost over the life of ownership (which isn't a big issue when you're flipping).

### Cash cow

The cash cow investor seeks to maximise passive income by only purchasing high-yielding property. This approach is usually seen to sacrifice capital gains in favour of high rental return, especially since most of these types of properties are in rural and low-population regional areas. A typical cash cow property will have a gross rental yield of 7 per cent or greater, but won't have any special features like a granny flat or multi-rooming options. Since these properties are often located in highly dislocated and low socio-economic areas, these types of properties can attract less-than-ideal tenants. This can result in additional maintenance and repairs, eroding the income that is earned.

A typical cash cow property may only cost an investor $200,000 to $250,000 but could be returning upwards of $7,000 to $10,000 in annual income after expenses.

Cash cow investors are usually seeking to grow their passive income in preparation for their lifestyle phase, but are not able to utilise the secondary dwelling strategy. The cash cow strategy can be very lucrative and effective in growing your passive income, but you must be careful to mitigate some of the risks that we have discussed.

### Secondary dwelling

The secondary dwelling strategy is another strategy that blends the active investor with the passive investor. A secondary dwelling, often referred to as a granny flat, is a small building usually located in the backyard of a property and is a fully self-contained residence. Often only consisting of one or two bedrooms, the granny flat will have a bathroom and kitchen, and is effectively a second house (albeit much smaller) on the one property. One of the big advantages of a granny flat is that you can build it on a property without having to subdivide or split the land (two topics that we cover later in this chapter). The downside is that there are still minimum land requirements to build a granny flat, and you also can't sell a granny flat separately from the main residence.

The main purpose for using the secondary dwelling strategy is for cash flow. As you can imagine, having a second house on your property means that you now have a second income stream. Although you won't receive anywhere near the amount of rental income as the main residence, granny flats could quite easily return an extra $300 to $500 per week. If an investor is seeking extra cash flow, a granny flat can be a fantastic opportunity to add further weekly income into the portfolio.

**Development**

Our final property strategy is development. Development is the most lucrative but also the riskiest strategy that we will cover. The concept of development can apply to a wide variety of activities; we will look at the most common types, as depicted in figure 5.2.

Figure 5.2: Common types of development

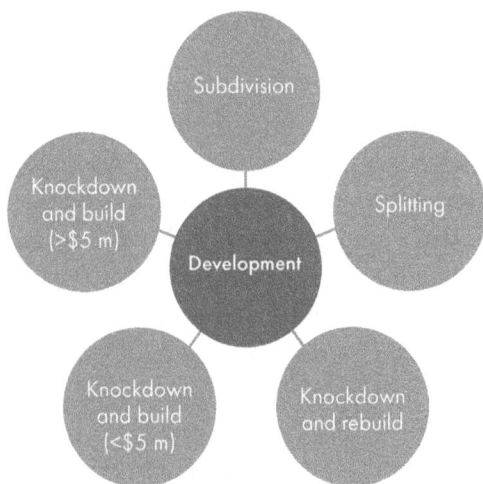

Our first type of development is subdivision. A subdivision is where you have a single plot of land that you divide into two smaller plots of land – see figure 5.3.

Every local council around Australia has different rules that govern when a subdivision is possible, however broadly speaking, land sizes greater than 800 m² have the best chance of being eligible. The benefits of subdivision are that you can divide the single plot into two smaller plots, thus increasing your ownership to two separate properties. You can then choose to hold the second plot of land, sell the land, or even build another property so that you then own two pieces of land that each have a house.

Figure 5.3: Subdivision

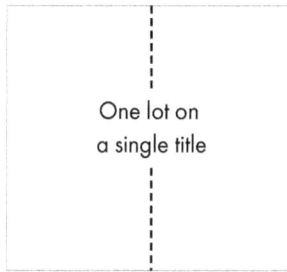

Table 5.16 shows some example figures for a small subdivision.

Table 5.16: Small subdivision example

|  | Value |
| --- | --- |
| Original property cost | $600,000 |
| Acquisition costs | $40,000 |
| Subdivision costs | $80,000 |
| Total costs | $720,000 |
| Original property – new value | $440,000 |
| New subdivided land – value | $350,000 |
| Total portfolio value | $790,000 |
| Net profit | $70,000 |

As you can see, there is massive value that can be created through subdividing property. Without even building a second house, this investor will have realised a profit of $70,000 which was through a predominately administrative process. If the investor decided to build a dwelling on their new piece of land, they could expect an even greater profit. The investor would then have the option to hold the property, sell the property or withdraw the equity and purchase another property.

Our second type of development is splitting. The difference between a splitter and a subdivision is that a subdivision occurs when a single plot of land is divided into two plots of land, whereas a splitter contains two plots of land on the title – the land is then 'split' across two titles rather than just existing on one (see figure 5.4). Splitters can be fantastic development opportunities because there is often less red tape in dividing up the titles than you commonly see with a subdivision. This is because the property is already split into two different plots of land – they have just been combined at some point in the past, often to build a bigger house and backyard.

**Figure 5.4: Splitter**

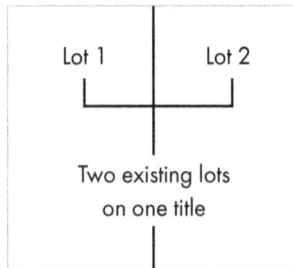

Lot 1        Lot 2

Two existing lots
on one title

Splitters are commonly seen in Brisbane, where you can find rectangular blocks of land of approximately 810 m² in size, which can then be split into their original 405 m² plots of land.

The third type of development is a knockdown and rebuild. Knockdown and rebuild is when you purchase an existing property (often in poor condition), knock it down and then rebuild a new property in its place. The knockdown and rebuild strategy can be very effective if you're an investor with some development experience under your belt and you're looking to take the next big step in your property journey. This strategy often relies on purchasing the worst house in the best street and then rebuilding it so that it can compete with the top properties on the market. A few big risks associated with this strategy are underestimating the demolition and construction costs, and building a home that is either overcapitalised or does not appeal to the wider market as much as you intended. Table 5.17 shows some example figures for a knockdown and rebuild.

**Table 5.17: Knockdown and rebuild example**

|  | Value |
|---|---|
| Property purchase | $350,000 |
| Acquisition costs | $30,000 |
| Demolition | $30,000 |
| New build | $250,000 |
| Holding costs | $15,000 |
| Total costs | $675,000 |
| New property value | $750,000 |
| Net profit | $75,000 |

As you can see, the knockdown and rebuild strategy can be profitable but does carry risk. Profit margins on knockdown and rebuilds for single houses are often much smaller than rebuilds for townhouses or apartments because you are creating less value (that is, you're building one house versus, say, three townhouses). Strong due diligence and worst-case-scenario planning are vital to ensure that a reasonable profit can be made from this type of development.

Our fourth development type is our knockdown and build (<$5 million). Since there are many types of developments that range from townhouses to low and high-rise apartments to residential estates, it's helpful to understand what can be achieved in the <$5 million bracket. This bracket is likely to be the maximum gross realisation value of any development that a typical investor will be able to undertake, mainly due to finance and development experience. Often, the typical investor won't come anywhere near to the top of the $5 million bracket, but it's a useful cut-off point for this strategy.

The focus of this strategy is to knockdown a pre-existing house (similar to the knock down and rebuild strategy), but instead of rebuilding another house, you add more value by constructing a small group of townhouses or an apartment building. By creating more value through additional dwellings on the land, greater returns can be made. Table 5.18 shows some example figures for a knockdown and build (<$5 million).

Table 5.18: Knockdown and build (<$5 million) example

|  | Value |
|---|---|
| Property purchase | $600,000 |
| Acquisition costs | $50,000 |
| Demolition | $30,000 |
| Build costs – four townhouses | $800,000 |
| Holding costs | $30,000 |
| Total costs | $1,510,000 |
| New property value | $1,800,000 |
| Net profit | $290,000 |

The example in table 5.18 shows how lucrative <$5 million developments can be. Unfortunately, this type of development often requires substantial amounts of cash for funding, which typical investors may not have at their disposal. In addition, complex loan arrangements and the requirement for commercial financing can add further layers of complexity for the average investor.

Our final strategy is the knockdown and build (>$5 million). This strategy is the most complex of all we have discussed and is usually only undertaken by a sophisticated investor. In this strategy, an investor will be a highly experienced developer who has access to significant capital as well as loan facilities for funding the development. This type of strategy will be out of reach for 99 per cent of people due to the complex finance requirements and significant development experience required.

While we would love to show you an example of the returns that could be achieved, the answer is endless. Since this type of development could be a new set of high-rise apartments or a large residential estate, the returns are hypothetically unlimited. The types of developments in this strategy will take several years to complete, require complex project management and involve sophisticated and intricate financing.

## MACRO FACTORS INFLUENCING THE PROPERTY MARKET

There are many different factors that affect the performance of property in Australia. We can broadly break these factors down into macro and micro factors. The big difference between macro and micro factors are that macro factors are widespread, such as across an entire state or country, whereas micro factors affect much smaller areas. Another common attribute of macro factors is that there is often very little you can do to influence them. Since we're talking about factors that may affect the entire country, often these are outside of your control and you have to do your best to make the most of how the factor is impacting your investing. We're going to cover some of the macro factors in this section, and you can learn about the micro factors in the next section.

### Access to credit

One of the most important macro factors for property investing is access to credit. Very few people purchase property without using a loan (otherwise known as credit), which means that if your access to credit is limited, so too is your ability to purchase property. The impact of credit availability was demonstrated throughout the 2010s, when government regulations limited the amount of money that could be borrowed using minimum interest rate assessment tests for loans. This meant that even if the loan you were attempting to secure had an interest rate of 4 per cent, most lenders were required to test your repayment ability at levels as high as 7 per cent or more. Ultimately, this curbed the ability of many investors and owner occupiers to acquire loans and slowed down a very hot property market. When some of these limitations were reduced in the late 2010s, access to credit improved and many property markets began to experience noticeable growth.

While there is very little the everyday investor can do to improve access to credit on a macro level, the ability to access credit is vital for property price growth.

### Consumer confidence

Consumer confidence is a vital aspect of the property market. While consumer confidence can be hard to measure, there are companies that regularly survey people from all backgrounds to understand how they feel about the current environment. Consumer confidence is important because without confidence, people won't feel comfortable spending money. If people think that their jobs are at risk or the economy is suffering, they are more likely to save their money and prepare for that rainy day. Conversely, when people feel comfortable and confident, they are more willing to make large discretionary purchases as well as spend money on essentials like housing. As an investor, understanding consumer confidence can give you a leg up – you can understand how the general population may be feeling about property and their willingness to enter the market, which drives up demand.

### Wage growth

If people don't have excess money from their salaries, it becomes exponentially harder for them to purchase property. Wage growth and inflation go hand in hand, and both are important to the property sector. Naturally, as inflation increases, wages must also increase, or people face a decrease in purchasing power. Wage growth and inflation also impact property prices because the cost of goods will increase over time, eventually flowing into the property sector where the prices of property will also increase – keeping pace with the true value of the dollar.

As wages grow, so too does people's ability to purchase property – particularly if wages are growing faster than the price of property. When people have more disposable income, they have a greater ability to spend money. This spending may be directly into a new property, but it also may be for improvements to properties currently owned. If everybody in a certain area has more disposable income and they all decide to complete small renovations to their properties, even those who don't renovate are likely to experience some capital growth in their properties. This is a great example of how wage growth can impact property prices.

### Government policy

Government policy is an incredibly important macro factor for property investors. Governments have the ability to make laws, regulations and best practices that can directly impact the demand for property. Negative gearing tax incentives have been a long-debated topic in Australia. Some people believe that the tax breaks that are available for those people who negatively gear property are unfair and that this area of taxation law should be closed. If the government ever decided to enact a change like this, there would be massive implications for the property market as many investors may decide that holding their investment properties is now unaffordable. This could then result in mass listings of properties for sale and a substantial drop in the value of properties as supply would far exceed demand. This situation is an example of how government policy can have wide-ranging impacts on property investors.

Another example of government policy related to property is stamp duty. There is a big push to abolish stamp duty in favour of annual property taxes, as governments believe this may improve housing affordability. If this were to occur, it is likely that substantially more people would enter the property market and this rise in demand would correlate into rises in property prices. While the government's intention is to improve housing affordability, it may actually hinder it as property values rise rapidly with the sudden influx of thousands of additional buyers.

Although we can't change government policy, we can understand what the likely impacts are. As you saw in the examples above, government policy can help property price growth or result in negative growth. It is important to understand each scenario and do your best to plan your reaction so that you can continue building and protecting your portfolio.

## MICRO FACTORS INFLUENCING THE PROPERTY MARKET

While macro factors have a broad impact across a state or even the whole country, micro factors affect a much smaller area, like a suburb or collection of suburbs. Micro factors are often the most-analysed factors, particularly at the suburb level. They are typically seen as the factors that can indicate future capital growth and rental growth. Like we mentioned with macro factors, there is no single micro factor that can determine a suburb's future performance, but an understanding and correct interpretation of macro and micro factors is pivotal in reducing risk and increasing investment performance. The micro factors that we are about to discuss are very important in determining future performance; however, there are other micro factors that exist, and we encourage you to continue your own education into them.

### Inventory

Inventory is perhaps the most important of all the micro factors we'll discuss. As we have mentioned previously, price growth is related to supply and demand. When there is more demand for properties than there is supply, prices will go up as people compete for a smaller pool of properties. This idea of supply and demand is best expressed through the inventory measurement. Quite simply, inventory is the amount of stock on market and is expressed in number of months – for example, 'there is three months of inventory on the market'.

While inventory is not a new concept in real estate on a global level, there has been limited use of it within Australia. Inventory is one of the most common measurements used in the United States – so much so that there are national bodies that write monthly reports based on inventory levels around the country. When looking at real estate investment data in Australia, there are other factors that are reported on at the expense of inventory – which we think is crazy!

To calculate inventory, you simply take the number of properties that are currently listed and divide it by how many properties typically sell per month. For example, if there are 50 properties listed for sale and there are typically 10 sales per month, then there is five months of inventory on the market.

While there is no magic number, it is generally accepted that six months of inventory translates to a balanced market. If there is less than six months, you have a market that should experience upward price pressure, and if there is more than six months, you will likely experience downwards price pressure. A sweet spot of two to three months of inventory typically implies that there is meaningful competition in the market and properties will experience reasonable capital growth.

**Days on market**
Our next micro factor is days on market. Days on market is another important measure of supply and demand because it shows how many days it takes for a property to sell. Combined with inventory, days on market is a powerful tool for evaluating the supply and demand characteristics of a suburb. If a suburb has a days on market

of 60, this is usually considered a balanced market. Below 60, there is expected to be additional competition in the market, and above 60 it is expected that there is less competition.

When viewed in conjunction with inventory, days on market can be thought of as how fast a property sells while inventory demonstrates how many properties are being competed for. If a certain market has two months of inventory and an average of 25 days on market, it would be expected that this suburb may be experiencing price growth as there is only two months of stock available and properties are being sold in only 25 days.

### Vacancy rate

Vacancy rate is an important tool for understanding the risk of investing in property. Vacancy rate is expressed as a percentage, and is a measure of how many properties in a suburb are currently vacant – that is, available for rent but not currently rented. A property is typically considered vacant when it has been on the market for rent for longer than 21 days. Thankfully, you don't need to trawl through listing portals and keep track of each property to determine the vacancy rate – there are plenty of data websites that keep track of the vacancy rates in each suburb.

It is commonly accepted that a vacancy rate of 3 per cent represents a balanced rental market. This means that a property is vacant for 1.5 weeks out of every year, which makes sense when you consider the time it takes for a tenant to move out of a property and a new tenant to move in. Vacancy rate is important for understanding risk because it gives an indication of an average period you may not be receiving rental income. In the 3 per cent example, this would mean that an investor would need to make sure they can cover that one-to-two-week gap in rental payments through other means, such as putting aside some rent from each month to cover any future income gaps.

## Past capital growth

Past capital growth can be an extremely divisive concept for property investors. On one hand, past performance is certainly no guarantee of future performance, but on the other hand, past performance can still tell us a story about an area. If an established area has data available for the last 30 years and it shows an average annual growth rate of 2 per cent, why would we suddenly expect it to perform at 10 per cent plus returns? It certainly could, but given the very large dataset and the fact that the area is established, there is no logical or statistical reason for such a large increase in returns.

Analysis of past capital growth should be considered with a very big grain of salt. As anybody who has worked with data knows, the larger and more reliable the dataset, the more reliable interpretations can be made. If you have a dataset that extends over 30 years, has limited outliers (such as multiple years of extreme growth or decline), is hyper-established and has no expected changes (such as massive infrastructure spending, natural disasters and so on), it may be reasonable to place at least some analytical value on past growth.

Historical capital growth is simply a tool in the experienced investor's toolkit. While we would never base assumptions or an investment on prior capital growth, if you have analysed a suburb through various macro and micro factors, the prior capital growth may become a common-sense check for the conclusion you had already arrived at. To reiterate, though, the data must be highly reliable – even for use as a common-sense check.

## Rental yield

Our final micro factor is rental yield. Rental yield is the annual rent expressed as a percentage of purchase price. If a property is rented for $500 per week, it would earn $26,000 per annum. If this property was purchased for $500,000, the rental yield would equal 5.2 per cent, found by dividing $26,000 by $500,000.

Rental yield is important as it gives an indication of whether a property will be positively or negatively geared. Particularly with interest rates as low as they are today, properties that have a rental yield of 4.5 per cent will often be positively geared. As suburbs move through the property clock (discussed in Step 4 – Professional mastery), rental yields will change. Rental yields are typically at their lowest when an area is at the top of the property cycle, and are often at their highest just prior to an area moving back into its peaking market.

There are countless asset types and market indicators that you can research to achieve excellence in your property investing. The best way to arm yourself in the property market is to research thoroughly and remain up-to-date with current trends and investing education. Through appropriate planning, constant personal development and research, you can give your personal investing strategy the best chance to be executed with military precision and effectiveness.

# Step 6:
# MISSION ANALYSIS

Achieving the mission is arguably the most important function of
the military. The mission itself will consistently change – it could be
anything from kinetic operations to humanitarian aid – but whatever
it is, achieving the mission is vital. To adequately prepare for every
mission, commanders will spend considerable time conducting a
mission analysis to better understand what they are required to
do and what constitutes mission success. This analysis is crucial,
otherwise commanders will fail to understand mission objectives
and the overall desired end state.

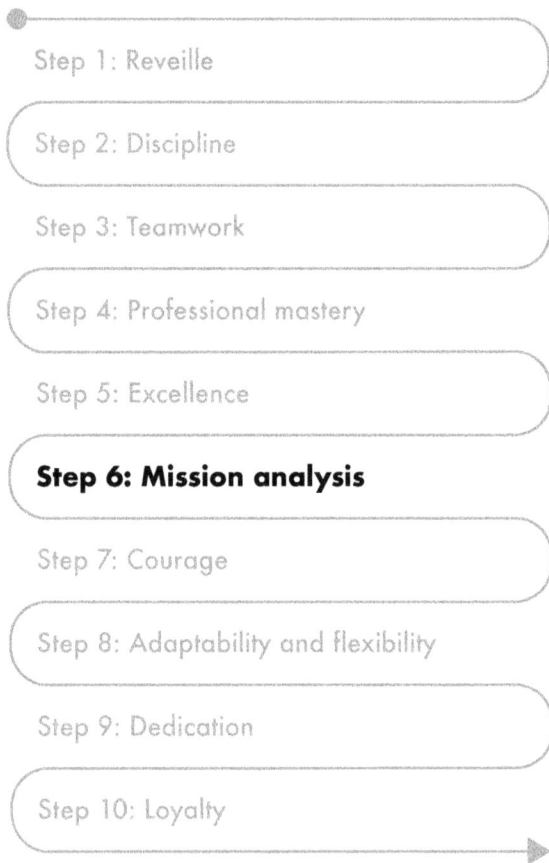

Step 1: Reveille

Step 2: Discipline

Step 3: Teamwork

Step 4: Professional mastery

Step 5: Excellence

**Step 6: Mission analysis**

Step 7: Courage

Step 8: Adaptability and flexibility

Step 9: Dedication

Step 10: Loyalty

## Step 6: Mission analysis

Effective mission analysis and planning has been key to the success of military operations for thousands of years. One operation that truly encapsulates the importance of mission analysis is Operation Jaywick, led by Special Operations Australia during World War II.

In September 1943, sailors and commandos from the Allied Z Special Unit (also known as Z Force) devised a cunning plan to attack Japanese ships that were located in the harbour of Japanese-occupied Singapore. A handful of British operators who also became a part of the Z Force had successfully escaped from Japanese-occupied Singapore and returned to Australia. Those British officers continued to work alongside the Australian Z Force members, who were selected from the Australian Army and Royal Australian Navy.

Z Force began to devise a plan to attack Japanese shipping in Singapore by analysing the experiences and intelligence that the British officers had collected during their time in the area. Z Force then began to meticulously train for the operation in remote areas of New South Wales in secret. A total of three British and 11 Australian personnel made up the deployed force for the mission and boarded their ship, named the *Krait*. On their voyage to Singapore, the team experienced unexpected damages to the tactical canoes that were stored onboard the ship. These canoes were critical to the mission's success since they were going to be used by Z Force members to covertly attach limpet mines to the Japanese ships under the cover of darkness. Luckily, the team was able to successfully adapt to the situation and undertake the repairs while underway to Singapore.

Nearly one month after departing Australia, the Z Force members paddled their canoes from their ship into the Singapore harbour and successfully placed multiple limpet mines onto several Japanese ships. They were then able to paddle back to their ship's hiding place and, after the commotion caused by the mine's explosions had passed, commence their return voyage to Australia.

It's estimated that Z Force was able to successfully damage or sink six Japanese vessels that night without ever arousing suspicion from the Japanese authorities in Singapore. The mission was a success and didn't result in any injuries or causalities of the Z Force members. This operation illustrates the importance of analysing the situation, conducting effective mission analysis, enacting adaptability when challenges arise and placing trust in thorough training. Although your personal investing journey will include starkly different activities to those undertaken by Z Force, there are countless lessons that you can take away from this example, which will be detailed in this chapter.

## THE ACQUISITION PROCESS

Each property purchase can be viewed as a different and unique mission on your journey to financial success. An important part of the property mission analysis includes understanding the general acquisition process, particularly if you have never purchased a property before. We're going to take you through the acquisition process so that there are no surprises as you embark on your journey. Keep in mind, every state and territory will have slightly different rules and it's important that you understand the specifics of the state that you are purchasing in. (A simplified purchasing checklist has also been included at the back of the book to act as a quick reference guide when needed!)

### Finance

For us, the first step in our mission is to gain our finance pre-approval. While you can purchase a property without a pre-approval, we prefer to receive pre-approval first because it gives us confidence that the lender should be willing to provide us a loan at the requested amount. Pre-approval can also be a negotiation tool – if you were an agent, would you rather accept an offer with pre-approval or one without?

The pre-approval process is relatively straightforward, especially when using the mortgage broker who is part of your trusted team, as recommended in Step 3 – Teamwork. Once a lender provides your pre-approval, you typically have 90 days before the pre-approval expires.

You might find that the amount of your pre-approval is lower than what you expect. This can be a difficult part of the process, particularly if it prices you out of your desired area.

Once you find your property and your offer is accepted, you will provide the lender with the specifics of the deal such as the location and price, and they will then provide an unconditional approval for your loan.

After you apply for your unconditional loan, the lender will undertake a valuation to ensure that you have not overpaid for the property. From their perspective, they don't want to provide a loan for a property that is worth much less than you are attempting to pay – if something goes wrong and they have to foreclose on the property, they won't be able to recoup their lost money if the property is worth substantially less than your offer.

Once the valuation is completed, the valuation will either come back at the purchase price or at a number below it. If the number is below it, you will have to either renegotiate the deal, pay the difference or walk away from the deal.

**Offer or auction**

Once you have your pre-approval and you've found the property, the offer or auction comes next. If the property is not listed for auction, it's time to place an offer. Again, every state and territory is different, but there are a few fundamental components to an offer. The offer is where you will list your price, settlement period and any special conditions. Typical special conditions include finance clauses, building and pest clauses, development clauses and property condition clauses. An offer is not binding until you place it on a formal contract and sign it.

If the property is listed for auction, there is nothing stopping you from submitting a pre-auction offer, but it will need to be very strong to stop the vendor moving to auction.

Auctions can be a very daunting experience, so let's break it down. There are two important things to know about an auction: firstly, often the person with the most money will win, and secondly, a win at auction means an unconditional contract. Prior to auction, you can receive a contract to review and then request that the vendor agrees to any conditions for your purchase – if you win the auction and the vendor agrees to any conditions, that's a big win for you! Otherwise, you are usually obligated to proceed with the contract as is and can't make any changes after the auction.

Before making any offer or bidding at an auction, we highly recommend having the contract reviewed by a legal professional such as a solicitor or conveyancer. By having the contract reviewed, you can be sure that there is nothing subtle or tricky in the fine print that puts you and your financial security at risk.

### Contract exchange

Our next stage is the contract exchange. As we just mentioned, if you win at auction, you are usually unconditional immediately, so this step is mainly applicable for those who have an offer accepted. Once you formally present a signed contract for sale to the vendor and they accept your offer and sign the contract, this is known as contract exchange. Congratulations, you're now only a few steps away from securing your investment! There are two main types of contract exchanges – conditional and unconditional.

A conditional contract exchange occurs when your offer is subject to certain conditions being met. A typical condition is that your offer is subject to finance approval from the bank. This means that if you don't receive your finance approval, you can exit the contract without incurring any penalties. Once all the conditions in the contract are met, you will be unconditional on your contract.

An unconditional contract exchange is much more straightforward. An unconditional contract exchange means that there are no conditions in the contract, and therefore there should be no reason for the contract to be exited by either party.

Regardless of your type of exchange, all contracts have a cooling-off period. This period varies based on location but is typically around three days, and allows you to exit the contract for any reason within this period for a small fee – typically 0.2 to 0.25 per cent of the contract price. For example, if you exchanged on a $500,000 property and decided to exit during the cooling-off period which incurs a 0.2 per cent fee, you would be required to pay the vendor $1,000.

**Building and pest inspection**
A building and pest inspection is a pivotal part of the acquisition process. It allows you to understand the condition of your future investment. A building and pest inspection is carried out by a licensed professional who inspects the whole property for any structural or pest-related issues. Depending on the market you are trying to invest in, this is usually done during the conditional contract exchange period or prior to giving an offer.

From a risk perspective, we would never purchase a property without a building and pest inspection because there are so many things that can't be seen by an untrained or naked eye. The last thing we would want is to purchase a property that has termites or is falling apart – we're sure you wouldn't want to do that, either!

If the inspection comes back with issues, this isn't the end of the world. Most established homes will have small issues here and there, but it is important to chat with the inspector to understand the risks and implications of each issue. If the issues are minor and you are still willing to proceed with the deal, you can even renegotiate with the vendor to either fix the problems or lower the price.

### Settlement

The final stage of the acquisition process is settlement. Thanks to advances in technology, settlement is now primarily done electronically and will be executed by your solicitor or conveyancer. Prior to settlement, you should ensure that you have completed a pre-settlement inspection to check the condition of the property and that all the previous owner's belongings and rubbish have been removed. Once the settlement has been completed, you are officially the owner of the property!

## PROPERTY VALUATION

Property valuation is often seen as a dark art, with many people worried about overpaying for property – especially investment properties. We are going to take you through the three methods used by property valuers who work for banks and valuation companies so that you can use the same tactics as the professionals.

As you learn about these methods, it's important to remember that property valuation is an art, not a science. Property valuation still relies on the subjective opinion of the valuer, and this can often result in tens of thousands of dollars' variation between two different valuers. Often, valuers will use at least two of the methods, with one of them being the primary valuation method and the other as a 'check' on their first method. The more you practise these approaches, particularly the comparable sales method, the better your valuation skills will become.

### Comparable sales method

Our first method, and by far the most common for residential property, is the comparable sales method. As the name suggests, this approach relies on comparing properties that are similar and have sold recently enough to still be appropriate to use. There is no hard-and-fast rule on the recency of the sale – in a hot market, you should be using properties no more than 4 to 6 months old, but a colder market can see sales extended out as far as 12 to 18 months.

When comparing properties, all features can be compared. Some of the common characteristics that a valuer will compare are the bedrooms, living spaces, kitchen, land size, land shape, location and even sales environment. The valuer will then assign one of three measures: inferior, similar or superior. After assigning a value to each characteristic of the property, a valuer will then give an overall comparison, again using one of the three measures.

Comparable sales is the most common valuation method because it uses real data (sales price) that shows how the public values similar properties. However, the method is still an art, because every property is different and unique, and it is up to your judgement on how much value you place upon one comparison to another.

**Summation method**

Our next method is the summation method. The summation method utilises the value of different parts of a property and combines them to give a valuation. The two components of the summation method are the land value and the improvements value. Improvements means anything that has been added to the land such as a house, pool, shed and so on.

The summation method can be easier to estimate when government land values of a particular property are easily accessible. To estimate the value of improvements, a valuer needs to take into account the age of the building, depreciation and cost of materials to rebuild to a similar standard. This can be difficult to estimate for the average person, but there are building manuals published annually that give estimates of building values – these can be used in place of uneducated estimates. Table 6.1 gives an example of a summation method valuation.

*Table 6.1: Example summation method valuation*

|  | Value |
|---|---|
| Land | $450,000 |
| Improvements | $400,000 |
| Total | $850,000 |

## Income method

The income method is widely used in commercial property valuation but is uncommonly applied to residential properties. We would only consider using the income method as another method to 'check' our first two methods of valuation – giving us more confidence in the valuation we have previously arrived at.

The income method utilises a figure known as the capitalisation rate. The capitalisation rate is similar to rental yield, except that instead of using annual rent it uses net operating income (NOI). Let's take a quick look at a calculation to break it down.

$$\text{Capitalisation rate} = \frac{\text{Net operating income}}{\text{Market value of property}}$$

To work out the NOI, you take the rent of the property and subtract all outgoings (council rates, management fees, maintenance and so on) but not the mortgage; you also subtract an allowance for vacancy. Table 6.2 shows an example.

*Table 6.2: Example net operating income calculation*

|  | Value |
|---|---|
| Annual rent @ $400 p/w | $20,800 |
| Less vacancy rate @ 3% | $624 |
| Total | $20,176 |

|  | Value |
|---|---|
| **Outgoings** | |
| Property management @ 8% | $1,664 |
| Council rates | $1,500 |
| Water rates | $800 |
| Maintenance | $1,000 |
| Total | $4,964 |
| Net operating income (NOI) | $15,212 |

There are two ways to proceed from here depending on the property information that you know. If you know the market value of the property, you can finish the equation by dividing the NOI by the market value and then compare the capitalisation rate of your property against other properties nearby. Alternatively, if you know the capitalisation rate of nearby properties and you are trying to work out the market value of your property, you can rearrange the equation:

$$\text{Market value of property} = \frac{\text{Net operating income}}{\text{Capitalisation rate}}$$

Using this re-arranged equation, you can now work out the value of your property (as per the example above):

$$\frac{\$15,212}{3.5\%} = \$434,628$$

A simpler approach for residential properties is to compare the rental yield of your property against the rental yield of similar properties. If your property has a rental yield of 5 per cent and similar properties have rental yields of 4.8 per cent, this doesn't necessarily mean your property is worth more since these yields are very similar for residential properties. However, if your property has a rental yield of 6.5 per cent and nearby properties are all renting for 4.5 per cent, this situation may be cause to consider whether your property is undervalued. Ultimately, in residential property, the income method should only be used in a common-sense fashion as its purpose is more closely aligned with commercial property.

## NEGOTIATION

One of the most important aspects of the acquisition process is the negotiation. Property investors don't make their money when they sell, they make their money when they buy. A poorly executed purchase that results in a property investor overpaying for their purchase can take years to make up for in capital growth. On the flip side, a property investor who makes a purchase below market value can have multiple years worth of equity built into the property from settlement.

The negotiation pyramid (figure 6.1) is a great tool for a successful negotiation. By working from the base up, you can create a strong negotiating environment that ensures you realise an excellent result and quality investment outcome.

*Figure 6.1: Negotiation pyramid*

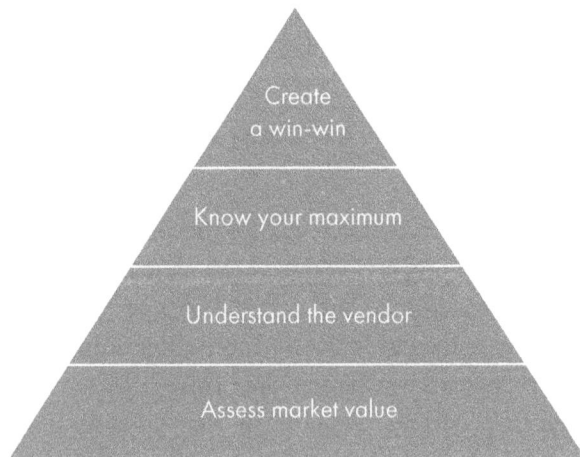

## Assess market value

The base of the pyramid and the most important step in an effective negotiating environment is to assess market value. By utilising the valuation techniques in this chapter, you will be able to assess the true market value of your target property, and this will form the basis of your negotiations.

Similar to how military personnel will carefully evaluate the value of their mission objective in the operating environment, investors must also examine their surrounds. If you don't know or properly understand what the market value of your investment is, how will you know if you have negotiated a good, fair or bad deal? If you don't understand the market value of the property, it will also be incredibly difficult to work out where to begin your negotiations and where you should walk away.

As you can see, assessing the market value of the property is critical to your success in negotiating a strong investment deal, which may result in equity being built into the property from your first day of ownership.

## Understand the vendor

The key to any good negotiation is understanding the other party. If you can understand the other party, you'll be able to understand their motivations for the transaction and possibly what their desired outcome is. Believe it or not, price is not necessarily the motivating factor in every property deal. Property owners can be motivated by many reasons, such as a desire for a quick sale, wanting to keep the sale private, needing to prolong the settlement, or a myriad of other reasons. By understanding the vendor, you may be able to offer terms that are favourable to their position but have a relatively minor impact on you.

Here are some examples of questions that you can ask to help understand the vendor:

- Why is the vendor selling?

- Does the vendor need a quick settlement?
- Does the vendor need an extended settlement?
- Is there anything I can offer other than price?
- Does the vendor have another property ready to move into or would they be interested in renting back?
- Would the vendor be motivated by a larger deposit?

### Know your maximum

Now that you have assessed the market value and you have an understanding of the vendor and their circumstances, it's time to work out what your maximum is. As we discussed earlier, price is not everything. When you evaluate what your maximum is, you also need to evaluate your maximum terms other than price. Some other terms to consider include settlement times, deposit percentage, repairs, and items to remain with the property.

At the end of the day, your primary reason for the purchase is investment. If you give too much in the negotiations, your property will be losing its investment return and you may end up with an underperforming property for years to come. For an investor, price is often the most important term to consider. A common example of an investor negotiating a great purchase price is by giving the vendor a quick or extended settlement – we've seen vendors willing to knock tens of thousands of dollars off the price!

### Create a win-win

Contrary to popular belief, the best negotiations are when all parties walk away feeling like they have won. Negotiating doesn't have to be a zero-sum game – which means that one person winning means another person *must* lose. We have seen many negotiations go south because one party came in too aggressively with no regard for the considerations of other parties in the deal. This can be a sure-fire way to annoy vendors and real estate agents and can kill all hope of achieving a deal, regardless of how much money you are willing to offer.

Thanks to your successful implementation of all the previous steps in the pyramid, you are in prime position to negotiate a win-win. By blending your maximum with the vendor's circumstances, you are now ready to ensure that you can negotiate a great investment result while the vendor still feels like they are able to achieve a win in their perception of the negotiations.

## PROPERTY MANAGEMENT

The due diligence and analysis required to purchase a property is very important, but a poor-quality property management team can quickly ruin a great investment. You should not underestimate the value of a strong property management team, particularly if you are time-poor or don't live locally to your investments. Let's take a look at the property management process (figure 6.2).

*Figure 6.2: Property management process*

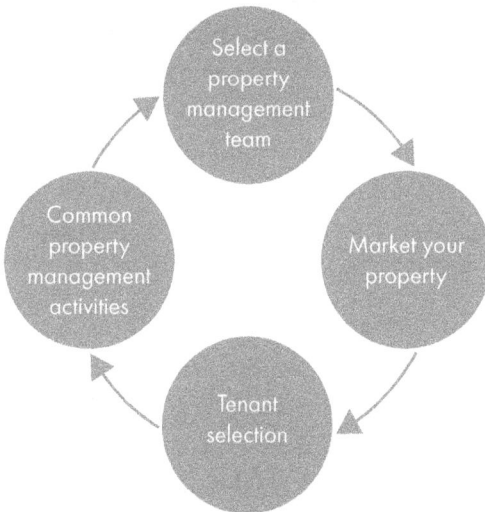

### Selecting a property management team

Selecting your property management team is one of the most important aspects of the property management process. Your property management team will have significant responsibility over your investment and will be the first point of contact for both you and your tenant. It is imperative that you select a team that you can rely on, because you will be trusting them to run your investment on your behalf in an efficient and effective way.

When seeking out a good property management team, it's important to interview each team you are considering. By interviewing each team, you'll be able to understand how they operate and the kind of service you can expect to receive. Here are some of the common questions we use to interview prospective property managers:

- How many properties does each property manager manage?
- What are your primary communication methods?
- What do you look for when assessing rental applications?
- What is your approach to problem resolution?

One of the most common things we hear investors querying is whether they should be going with the team that has the cheapest property management fee. Our approach is that you get what you pay for in property management. During your interviews, it's important to get a feel for how the team operates so that you can attach a value to them. After you've interviewed all the prospective teams, you will need to use your judgement to decide on a team that you feel represents the best value, regardless of cost.

### Marketing your property

Now that you've decided on your property team, it's time to market your property. Property marketing is a skill, and your property management team should demonstrate excellence in this area of the process. The two key parts of this process are the rental amount and the advertising. Based on your analysis during acquisition, you will already have a firm idea of the expected rental return for the property. Your property management team will be able to give you expert local advice on how to market the property to achieve your minimum acceptable rent or a higher amount.

Depending on the rental market at the time, you may not need to spend significant amounts of money on advertising due to high demand for your property. The professional advice of your property manager will be key in deciding your level of advertising, but don't be afraid to spend a few hundred dollars more if you feel that is what is required in the current market.

### Tenant selection

Tenant selection can be the make-or-break factor that decides whether an investment is successful and low-maintenance or requires constant attention and money. Tenant selection is one area where property managers earn their keep and provide invaluable experience. Assuming that you've bought a well-located property in a tight market, it would be reasonable to expect multiple tenancy applications once you advertise the property. Tenant selection is certainly an art and not a science, as there are so many variables that can impact on your decision. Ultimately, you want to ensure that you select a tenant who has a demonstrated record of timely rental payments and no incidences of poor behaviour or damage to a property. Your property manager will be invaluable in reducing the list to only the most appropriate tenants before involving you in the process.

### Common property management activities

You've now selected a fantastic tenant and they've moved into the property – unfortunately this isn't the end of the property management process. The process continues 365 days a year, but a good property manager will ensure that your time and input is required as little as possible.

Some of the typical activities you can expect to see occurring over a 12-month period include:

- rental disbursements
- property inspections
- maintenance requests
- general tenant enquiries.

Depending on your property management agency, rental disbursements will typically occur on a fortnightly or monthly basis. You will usually receive the rent minus management fees and any other expenses that have arisen over the period.

Your property manager will conduct regular property inspections on your behalf. Depending on the location of your property, this may be as many as three or four per year, but will typically only be one or two. Inspections are a crucial part of the property management process as they are one of the few times your property manager can check in on the condition of your property. It's important that both you and the property manager take inspections seriously, as these will usually be the times that you are able to see if the tenants are treating your property with care and respect.

As time passes, properties will require both routine and unexpected maintenance to keep the building in a quality condition. Your property manager will liaise with you regarding all maintenance that may be required. These may be small annual tasks such as smoke alarm compliance, or they could be as large as major repairs if something occurs. You should look to balance maintenance costs to ensure you don't spend thousands every year on minor details but don't shy away from fixing issues that could become bigger problems if left unrepaired.

Finally, your property manager will be the first point of contact between the tenant and yourself. A good property manager will be able to differentiate between legitimate tenant requests and some of the less-legitimate enquiries. Tenants can either be stress-free and uncomplicated in nature or extraordinarily difficult. Ideally, you have selected a quality tenant during the selection phase, but sometimes people can slip through the cracks. It is important to try to be accommodating and helpful to your tenants, as they are taking care of your investment; however, it is also important to know your boundaries on what you are willing to provide for the tenant. Some common examples of tenant requests are pay TV installation, pet requests, updating fixtures and fittings, and garden upkeep. When assessing tenant requests, always remember that they are trying to make a home for themselves, but don't be afraid to balance the cost against your return – it is an investment after all!

There is a lot to unpack when we analyse the mission of property investing. From valuing the property to understanding the acquisition process, there is a lot to know to ensure that you can undertake your mission safely and successfully. Half the battle when preparing for a new mission is ensuring that you analyse it properly, otherwise you may find yourself prepared for a different mission to the one you are presently undertaking. Our best advice to you is to ensure that you thoroughly analyse each individual part of the mission, and if you're struggling during the process, seek help from one of your trusted team members.

# Step 7:
# COURAGE

Courage in the face of fear and adversity is learned and enacted almost daily by serving military members. Those who display the highest levels of courage in combat have their bravery recognised through honourable decorations, including Australia's most prestigious military honour, the Victoria Cross. For a majority of personnel, courage is shown daily in many other ways – whether it be waving goodbye to their family and friends as they sail away with their ship's company for a nine-month deployment to the Middle East, or comforting a local whose life has been changed forever after a devastating flood or bushfire.

Step 1: Reveille

Step 2: Discipline

Step 3: Teamwork

Step 4: Professional mastery

Step 5: Excellence

Step 6: Mission analysis

**Step 7: Courage**

Step 8: Adaptability and flexibility

Step 9: Dedication

Step 10: Loyalty

## Step 7: Courage

It takes courage and commitment to step into the unknown, take control of a situation and conquer fear while inspiring those around you to do the same. In this chapter, we apply these lessons to taking control of your investing and your financial future.

There is no denying that taking control of your financial future will take courage, and lots of it. If you asked every Australian the question, 'Would you like to achieve financial freedom before you retire?' you'd be hard-pressed to find anyone who would answer no.

We already know that the majority of Australians desire financial security. This security comes in many forms, including the choice to have multiple holidays a year, or the decision to create a form of passive income to supplement your salary so you don't have to work a standard five-day working week. However, there is one substantial reason as to why most people will never achieve financial freedom: they refuse to take the courageous leap that is necessary to break into the investment market.

### COURAGE PAYS OFF

According to the Australian Taxation Office (ATO), there are just over 2.2 million property investors across the country. This means that approximately 20 per cent of Australians own an investment property and the other 80 per cent do not. Believe it or not, this aligns with a common phenomenon known as the Pareto principle. The Pareto principle states that 80 per cent of outcomes result from only 20 per cent of causes. We see this in global wealth distribution where 80 per cent of the world's wealth is controlled by the top 20 per cent of the richest people.

Back to the ATO statistic – these numbers confirm several trends to us. First, 20 per cent of Australians have taken a commendable leap and broken into the property market. This is no easy feat, and we congratulate any investor for taking the first step towards building a property portfolio that can successfully generate scalable capital gains and rental income. However, this statistic also highlights the fact that a significant majority of Australians are not choosing property as their trusted wealth-creation vehicle. According to the 2020 ASX Australian Investor Study, 9 million (or 46 per cent of) Australian adults have chosen to adopt investments outside of their super and their primary place of residence (see figure 7.1). Already, we can see that 54 per cent of the Australian adult population are simply not investing and will be relying upon their super or paid pensions once they retire. From this, we can conclude that these people will most likely not be achieving the levels of financial freedom that people like us desire.

### Figure 7.1: Investing in Australia

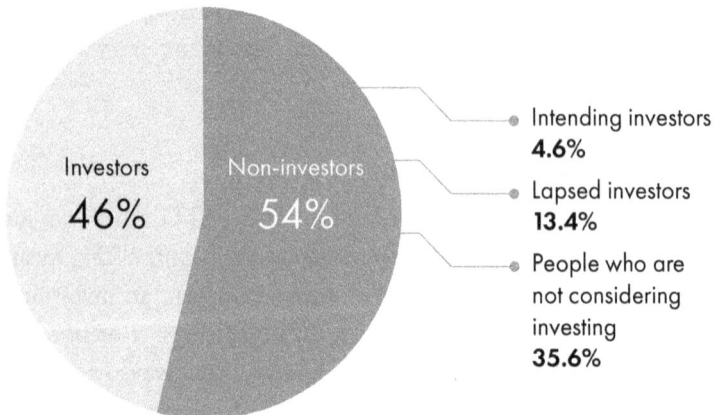

Source: Australian Securities Exchange (2020)

So, you might be asking yourself, 'Where are the 46 per cent of Australians who are investing currently putting their hard-earned cash?' According to the ASX, over half of these 9 million adults are investing in shares, which renders shares a primary wealth-creation vehicle of choice for a majority of Australian investors.

Although there are numerous advantages associated with investing in shares, their popularity can be explained by several key characteristics of the asset class. First, buying shares is extremely accessible. Thanks to our laptops and smartphones, the ASX and other international stock exchanges can be accessed in seconds via numerous brokerage sites and applications. Unlike property investing, shares have a much lower barrier to entry and don't require a sizeable deposit in the same way as a property. As a result, any adult with a smartphone, a bank account and a few hundred dollars can officially call themselves an investor as soon as they purchase their first stocks. Now, we aren't discouraging those who invest in shares. A fair portion of our own personal investment portfolio is made up of shares, and we certainly wouldn't be where we are today without the profits that we have made from this asset class. However, just like property investing, shares also require a considerable amount of research into each particular company and its associated industry. Shares also carry significantly more risk than property, as measured by their higher levels of volatility. This means that as quickly as a share's value can escalate, it can easily go down just as fast.

Secondly, as we discussed in Step 2 – Discipline, those who invest in shares will not reap the same leverage benefits as those who invest in property. Although shares can achieve growth percentages that are rarely seen in the property industry, properties (in an average to well-performing suburb) can provide 4 to 9 per cent annual growth for as long as they are held. According to the RBA, Australian property on a national scale has increased in value by 7.25 per cent per annum over the past 30 years. If a property investor held onto a property that was purchased 30 years ago for a purchase price of $100,000, that property would now be worth $816,430. This is because of the power of leverage that the investor has utilised from the property. This power of leverage becomes even more significant when you realise that there are numerous lenders available who will accept 10 per cent deposits for residential property purchases. Using the $100,000 property example, $816,430 for a $10,000 deposit becomes increasingly impressive. Although this growth on the property takes time and a semi-significant investment in the beginning, the growth is stable, reliable and less volatile than what an investor may typically encounter on the stock exchange.

So, what's the conclusion we're drawing from all of this? Although the barrier to enter the property market is substantially higher than other asset classes such as shares, we advocate for all investors to take a leap of courage and decisive action to incorporate property into their personal portfolio. Shares and similar investments can be excellent asset classes in their own right, however we advocate for property because of the leverage, reliability and stability it provides investors for their money. At the end of the day, demand for housing is continuously increasing in line with inflation and population growth, and Australians will always require homes to live in. This is why we stress the importance of supply and demand in every asset class that we assess for its investment potential.

## ARE YOU AN INVESTOR OR A SPECULATOR?

To ensure you're in the correct mindset for the property game, it is useful to reflect upon whether or not you consider yourself to be an 'investor' or a 'speculator'. Do you have the ability to be courageous in the market without wading into overly risky waters? We're going to evaluate the definitions of each; as we do, take the time to critically evaluate yourself and your current investing strategy or plan. To do so will take a level of dedication and introspection, so ensure that you're honest with yourself.

An investor is characterised as someone who aims to generate profits or income by understanding and balancing the risk versus the return of an investment. Appropriately balanced investments are attained by investors through conducting adequate amounts of research, performing fundamental analysis, studying trends and patterns, and defining their investment portfolio with a well-thought-out strategy. Investors also investigate financing options available to them and make use of lenders and brokerage services in order to align their portfolio with their goals and accepted levels of risk tolerance.

Speculators, on the other hand, are not well-advised and quite often find themselves with less money at the end of their investment journey than what they started with. Speculators are known for putting their money into investments that quite often fail and/or don't generate positive returns. Speculators would rather put all of their hard-earned cash into endeavours that are labelled 'high and fast returns' because they are not as knowledgeable or experienced in understanding the risk versus the reward.

Speculators will also try to source investments that do not have to be held for a significant amount of time to turn a profit. Speculators want to make their money quickly and swiftly exit the investment so they can put their money back into the 'next big winner'. An example of this type of investment is shares in the latest and greatest technological-based company, where the chances of the share price skyrocketing are just as high as the chances of the company plummeting into bankruptcy. In this situation, an investor would do their research and quickly turn their backs on the new start-up because the risk is far greater than the reward. However, a speculator would rarely perform their market research and is easily swindled into these types of advertised returns.

As you can see, it almost takes more fearlessness (or stupidity) to be an ill-advised speculator and invest in high-risk endeavours that repeatedly fail. In this guide, we're not asking you to find the courage to risk your hard-earned cash on an investment that's likely to result in losses – we are simply asking you to have the mental fortitude and dedication to conduct your own research and formulate your own investment strategy required to achieve financial freedom.

## WANTING MORE FOR YOURSELF...

No-one will ever want more for yourself than you. Your family and friends may wish you nothing but the best, but no-one is going to do the hard work or the research for you.

Building a better financial future for yourself has never been more important. According to the Association of Superannuation Funds Australia, over 57 per cent of retirees will have to partially or substantially rely on the Age Pension as of 2023 due to a lack of adequate savings. This means that only 43 per cent, well under half of those who wish to retire, will be sufficiently self-funded through their own assets, superannuation and investments. To think that not even half of Australian retirees in the near future will have the financial independence to live a comfortable and carefree life in their golden years is staggering. Let this be the motivation you need to dedicate your time and effort to building a more financially secure life for yourself and your family in the coming decades.

As we discussed in Step 1 – Reveille, only you hold the key to your financial future. By no means are we saying that planning a roadmap to your own financial success is easy. We have all feared the morning that we decide to sit ourselves down and take a hard look at our personal spending habits to create a new and better household budget. Many people find this simple task to be quite scary and daunting. Sometimes you might feel fearful or angry at yourself at the lack of progress that you think you have made when it comes to your finances. Perhaps you've once sat down with your latest bank statement and thought to yourself, 'I have worked at my current job for three years and I have no savings, assets or investments to show for it,' or, 'I thought I'd be able to save more after I secured that promotion, but now I'm just spending more on my lifestyle.'

This can be a hard pill to swallow, and trust us, we've been there before. Taking control of your financial future will take courage and personal reflection. This can certainly feel daunting, but it is your first step towards demanding more of yourself and your financial future.

## ... AND THE CONSEQUENCES OF NOT WANTING MORE

While it will be hard to enact a plan, it becomes much easier once you take a look around and glimpse the lives of those who have actively chosen to live a financially insecure lifestyle. We have all seen friends or family members choosing to spend their paycheques as frivolously and extravagantly as they please. These people always seem to have the latest iPhone, the most expensive laptop, a third round of cocktails at dinner or a brand-new car that they bought for themselves as a treat.

Lack of financial discipline is also demonstrated in smaller ways. For example, take someone who chooses to buy two coffees, a cafe lunch and a takeaway dinner every working day. This example isn't too hard to fathom, and many of us probably know a handful of these types of people at work or within our friendship groups (or you might be that person yourself!). Let's add up the cumulative total of these purchases. We'll assume that a medium coffee costs $4.50, a cafe lunch $12.50 and takeaway dinner $25. Ten coffees, five lunches and five dinners quickly totals to $232.50 per week. When we multiply that total by 52 for every week of the year, we reach a grand total of $12,090.

Now, we understand that we all have to eat and there's certainly room in life for a few social coffees. But imagine if that person had chosen to limit their coffee to two a week, buy their own groceries, and cook lunches and dinners at home for the working week for $5 per serving, rather than spending an average of $46.50 per working day at the cafe or nearest takeaway store?

They would quickly lower their weekly total of $232.50 to $59.00 by eating 10 meals at $5 per serving and choosing to limit themselves to two cafe coffees a week. This saves them $173.50 per week, totalling to $9,022 a year. Simple life choices quickly compound, and over a period of just four years, these small changes can create a domino effect and quickly turn into an investing cash pot. After just four years (minus any additional savings or investing efforts) a lump sum of $36,088 will be saved, which could be enough to fund a deposit for some investors and first home buyers. This example illustrates a concept also known as the aggregation of marginal gains, which we learned about in Step 2 – Discipline.

## WHAT IT MEANS TO BE FINANCIALLY FREE

It's considerably harder to make active change in our lives when we're unsure of the outcome that we are striving for. Although there are countless reasons as to why someone would choose to invest, we recommend that you aim for one overarching and superior end state: the goal to achieve financial freedom.

Financial freedom means having enough cash, investments and assets to allow you to build the life that you envision for yourself and your family. Ultimately, financial freedom allows you to have one key ability in life: the ability to choose. Choice is a privilege that the wealthy certainly have over those who are not financially free. The financially free have the choice to not work five days a week. The financially free have the choice to go on holidays multiple times a year, and have the choice to set up their children for their futures.

We all have one singularly finite resource that is required to secure our financial futures, and that finite resource is time. As financially secure people come closer to achieving financial freedom in their lives, they no longer have to trade their time for their income. This is because their investments are working for them in an independent and concurrent fashion and are reaping the benefits of compounding growth over time. This is the ultimate goal that we envisage for all of our readers and clients, and it's a goal that we encourage you to strive for.

To achieve such a goal will take time and commitment. Notice how the end state is also not strictly prescriptive. We aren't recommending that you go out and purchase four investment properties or build a portfolio with a particular percentage of commercial and residential properties in order to achieve financial freedom. Every investor's portfolio is going to look completely unique. If you choose to prescribe yourself to an end state that will help you achieve an element of financial independence and security, it doesn't matter what your method (your portfolio) looks like. As long as the investment is sound in quality and follows the fundamentals that we laid out in Step 4 – Professional mastery and Step 5 – Excellence, you'll be on your way to achieving success. This includes actively making the small, incremental but necessary changes to your budget and spending habits to facilitate the accumulation phase of your investment portfolio. As detailed in Step 2 – Discipline, the aggregation of marginal gains is crucial to this step.

It will take courage and commitment to implement these changes, even if it appears easy in practice. But those who take this step will be well on their way to reaping the rewards of their hard work.

## PROPERTY INVESTING IS INHERENTLY RISKY

Every operation that our soldiers, sailors and airmen and airwomen deploy on will carry an element of risk. However, if the mission's outcome renders the risk acceptable, the mission is always prioritised.

It's undeniable that any form of investment, from residential property to Bitcoin, will carry a probability or likelihood of incurring a loss relative to the expected return. To counter this risk, due diligence and thorough research is required by every investor before they put their hard-earned cash into any form of investment. Some investors even adopt a mantra of 'don't invest any amount of money that you're not willing to lose'. Although this is a wise goal to adopt, it's not always achievable for most. Say you're about to purchase your first investment property for $350,000. It's highly unlikely that you have a spare $350,000, or even another 10 per cent deposit, available in your pocket to completely counter the risk you're adopting. But luckily for us property investors, residential property carries significantly less volatility and uncertainty than most other investment classes.

A more realistic view of risk in property is accepting the fact that your portfolio may not generate a profit every single year. This is an unavoidable reality in the cyclic nature of the property cycle. Market growth continuously fluctuates, and unless you're a buyer who intends to watch the market incredibly closely and attempt to predict market downfalls in order to sell your property before incurring any losses, it's likely that your properties will experience a few phases of neutral or negative growth. But this is completely normal. Always remember that the most important days in the market are the day you buy and the day you sell. During the time in between these two days, as long as your suburb incurs more years of growth than decline, your property should be achieving an investment return.

Other key risks and challenges that property investors will inevitably face will be detailed in Step 8 – Adaptability and flexibility. For now, understand that there are risks in property that lie outside of the general market risk. These risks include those posed by tenants, the property itself (that is, damage and repairs), the threat of natural disasters, changes to interest rates, legislative risk, inflation risk and more. Similar to any mission, steps can be taken to actively minimise your exposure to risk, but you can never truly remove all risk. As long as you enter your investing journey with an aware and well-researched mindset, you'll be as prepared as you can be to minimise your portfolio's exposure to uncertainty.

As we alluded to in Step 3 – Teamwork, achieving success is much easier when you're surrounded by people who share your passion and vision. Those who achieve financial freedom rarely do so alone. They consistently make an effort to surround themselves with subject-matter experts who are leaders in their industry. They also find their own crowd that shares similar goals and hopes for the future. It is much easier to envision your own success if you are supported by encouraging, reassuring and like-minded people who won't attempt to dismiss your endeavours or deter you from achieving your end state. If you engage with others who attempt to derail your efforts due to intimidation or jealousy, you'll find yourself needlessly distracted or even questioning your own objectives.

This is why it is essential to find your crowd and stick with them. You must dedicate your time to building a team that supports you and your endeavours while you do the same for them. Courage isn't so hard to find when you share a strong sense of mutual trust and respect, and share values with those around you. Until you do, have the courage to stand alone and forge your own path to financial freedom.

# Step 8:
# ADAPTABILITY AND FLEXIBILITY

In the military, learning to be adaptable and flexible in dynamic environments is crucial. While on operations, military personnel are taught how to instinctively react if the worst were to happen. We train, drill and practise until contingency becomes our norm.

Step 1: Reveille

Step 2: Discipline

Step 3: Teamwork

Step 4: Professional mastery

Step 5: Excellence

Step 6: Mission analysis

Step 7: Courage

**Step 8: Adaptability and flexibility**

Step 9: Dedication

Step 10: Loyalty

## Step 8: Adaptability and flexibility

There's a well-known saying in the military: 'No plan ever survives first contact.' This is where adaptability and flexibility are essential. If every military force believed that their plan would be successful, there would be far more decisive victories written into history. However, we know this isn't the case. Victories can be challenging and messy, often requiring dynamic thinking and swift, adaptable actions. The battles that make it into history are those where the force was flexible in overcoming the challenge and adapting in creative ways.

Adaptability and flexibility are fundamental skills that play a critical role in Australian military operations and training programs. Serving members of the ADF know that the training areas where we conduct our annual exercises are starkly different to the terrain, climate and conditions experienced overseas when we deploy. The environment experienced by troops on the ground in the Middle East will differ greatly to those encountered in training areas, and strait transits conducted by a ship's company in contested waters will feel much more stressful than transits conducted in our own exclusive economic zone.

The aim of our military training isn't to work so hard that the operational environment we deploy in doesn't matter; rather, the aim is to adapt our mindset, methodologies and equipment to fit into the new environment as best as possible.

When it comes to deployments, personnel are provided with an opportunity to implement their training and skills in real scenarios that contribute to the nation's overarching mission. But a government doesn't send its troops straight into an operational environment from training units without the necessary preparation. This is where pre-deployment training and 'workups' come in. These provide soldiers, sailors and airmen and airwomen with the opportunity to practise their skills, adapt their mindset and prepare for the challenges ahead. This plays a critical part in both personal and team-based preparation.

Overall, military personnel who are well practised in adaptability and flexibility will consistently outperform those who fail to adapt to the dynamic operational environment. Being flexible to change and unforeseen challenges in the tactical environment is absolutely critical to success, and we're going to show you how these traits can also be utilised in the investing world.

## SETBACKS IN INVESTING

Similar to military operations, there will be setbacks on your investing journey. The question is, do you let the challenge overcome you, or do you overcome the challenge? Implementing adaptability and flexibility within your personal investing journey will enable you to bounce back whenever the unexpected happens. Whether you lose a deal because the owner accepted a different offer, or unexpected damage occurs to your property that requires urgent and costly repairs, setbacks are a part of every investor's journey. Although there will be setbacks, this also means you have opportunities to make the best out of challenging situations and remain focused on the end goal – achieving your version of financial freedom.

We're going to take a deep dive and analyse some of the most common challenges that property investors face, and methods to implement adaptability and flexibility during these times. But first and foremost, we recommend to all investors that you accept the fact that you will face challenges on your journey. The only remedy is to be as prepared as possible.

Methods of preparation are unique to each investor, but a few of our personal approaches include:

- having a reasonable emergency fund for each dwelling
- developing and maintaining excellent relationships with property managers

- paying for necessary insurances
- keeping a finger on the market pulse so you can enter and exit the suburb's property cycle at the most advantageous stages to attain growth.

Like all investment classes, there are risks associated with owning property, but the risk versus reward trade-off is a lot stronger with property than other asset classes. If you're overly worried about these risks, property may not be the asset class for you; other investments such as bonds may be your cup of tea. But for those who are set on realising the benefits that property can generate for your portfolio, let's take a look at some key challenges and how best to overcome them through adaptability and flexibility.

## CHALLENGES WHEN YOU MISS OUT ON PROPERTIES

One of the main challenges that we see prospective buyers struggling with is that they are consistently missing out on properties. This challenge is more commonly experienced in a hot market where market supply is low, buyers are motivated and investors are keen to get their slice of the pie. When you keep missing out on properties that you have invested so much time, due diligence and research into, it can be difficult to stay motivated and you may think about quitting the search for good.

Sometimes in property you can conduct all of the right research, look in all the right suburbs and prepare the best offer possible for the vendor, and still miss out. Property is a cutthroat game, and if the market conditions are right, you certainly won't be the only one searching for a great investment! If competition in suburbs that you're researching is tight and you continue to fall short of closing the deal, there are several approaches that you can use to increase your chances of securing a great outcome.

Firstly, this is a time for self-reflection. We don't mean that it's time to reflect on whether property investing is for you! We mean that you need to reflect on your actions on a tactical level and analyse what's working and not working in your favour.

### Being priced out of the market

There are lots of reasons why you could be continuously missing out on securing your chosen properties, but the most common is a lack of money. In competitive markets, investors commonly find themselves priced out of the market because other prospective buyers simply have more cash than them. This can be a frustrating realisation to make, but if listing agents are consistently informing you that your offer has been rejected because other investors have offered more, that might be an indication that you're getting priced out of that particular suburb or dwelling type.

**Solution:** Being adaptable during these times is crucial so you don't keep missing out on properties. If you're consistently being priced out of properties, there are three key solutions that you can implement:

- widen your search area
- look for properties at a lower price point
- gather more cash so you can submit a more competitive offer.

Widening your search area or looking into completely new areas of the market can help you find high-performing properties at a price bracket that better suits you. This will enable you to submit competitive and attractive offers to vendors, which will greatly increase your likelihood of success.

Searching for properties at a lower price point can also help, but you also need to ensure that the dwellings at that lower price point still have all of the elements that you've analysed as being in demand by the suburb's demographic. For example, if the suburb has a high percentage of families that contain four or more people, a three or more bedroom house would likely be in high demand by the suburb's occupants. In this circumstance, searching for a dwelling with one less bedroom in order to lower your price point may not be a great tactic, because you would be sacrificing an inherent element of the property that is in high demand.

Instead of searching for a dwelling with fewer rooms, you could search for properties with a smaller land size or more dated interior to save on the price tag. All successful investors will still need to acquire properties with characteristics that are desired by the suburb's demographic. Ensure you complete your research when it comes to lowering your price point, and if you can't enact enough flexibility to make the price point work without having to sacrifice key characteristics of the property, then it's time to start researching in a different market.

## When something is 'always wrong'

We see a lot of keen investors who seem to find problem after problem with potential investments. Whether it's the style of the garden, a dated bathroom, a handful of required repairs or an old stove cooktop, some investors are simply turned off whenever they view properties that aren't perfect or don't meet their specific 'vision'. No matter how many properties these investors inspect, they just aren't sold on any of them. This results in a lot of missed opportunities, personal frustration, annoyed agents and wasted time that could've been spent in the market gaining tangible growth.

As discussed in earlier steps, we personally subscribe to a property strategy that includes established houses that have been around for the past one, two or three decades. These houses provide plenty of opportunities, including renovation, subdivision, medium to high-density development and high demand from families. This is our tried-and-tested strategy, and it works.

It can take some investors a lot of time to realise that their investment properties are simply that – investments. You, as the investor, will never have to live in that property or conform to the lifestyle that the property or location prescribes. The dwelling doesn't have to meet your personal tastes and it certainly doesn't have to be perfect. As long as you've conducted your market research and there is demand for that particular location and dwelling type, then somebody out there will want to rent it.

**Solution:** There is an overarching strategy that allows investors to remain focused on their investment goal while remaining flexible in the market, and that strategy is to remain *unemotional*. When you take the emotion out of investing, all you are left with is data to analyse and interpret. If you crunch the available data and your calculations demonstrate that the property can generate a great return for your portfolio, then you have all the reason you need to invest. But if you continue to trust your emotions and fail to be adaptable and flexible to potential investment opportunities, you'll continue missing out in the market.

For example, let's say you go out to inspect a house in a suburb that you've analysed, and you believe the suburb is about to experience a solid growth period. The house has three bedrooms, two bathrooms and two car parks on an 800 m² block and meets the requirements for the suburb's family-based demographic.

On closer inspection, the property looks like it will need some work in the future. The kitchen and both of the bathrooms will require renovations in coming years, and the carpets could also be replaced. The garden in the backyard also looks considerably overgrown, so a professional gardener could probably be engaged to spruce up the property before having tenants come through and inspect it. All in all, the house has excellent bones and requires no major repairs.

Rather than turning your nose up and thinking negatively about the property – 'This place is completely dated; I certainly wouldn't want to live here,' or 'This place looks like it needs a lot of work in coming years; I'd rather have a turn-key investment where I don't have to get my hands dirty' – you should think of these challenges as opportunities. The dated nature of the property will certainly be reflected in the price, so you could possibly pick yourself up a bargain and generate considerable rental yield. Additionally, the house may have both renovation and subdivision potential, depending on the zoning. Overall, you shouldn't have any mathematical or logical reason as to why the house wouldn't make a fantastic investment. So rather than rely on your emotion-based assessment of the house, you should look at the opportunity through an investment-based lens and choose to consider the option more carefully.

Ensure that you conduct your due diligence and crunch the numbers to see what could generate excellent rental yield and capital growth opportunities. Remember that these properties will never be homes that you intend to live in – this is why it is so important for investors to separate their searches for owner-occupier and investment properties. Your search should strictly be business-focused and numbers-focused. As soon as you get emotional, you're likely to make more mistakes and become unadaptable to opportunities that could be sitting right in front of you.

If you're the type of investor who can't remove emotion from property investing or would like to gain some additional guidance from a professional, you may want to consider engaging a buyer's agent (BA). As we learned in Step 3 – Teamwork, an investment-focused BA is skilled in identifying high-performing suburbs, sourcing investment-grade properties and crunching the data that's required to analyse whether the property is suited to your financial goals. And the best bit? They're completely impartial to the design and location of the property. BAs are able to provide you with unbiased, well-researched and high-quality investment options so you don't have to do the research and data-crunching yourself.

### Analysis paralysis and passive approach

Inaction can occur due to two different reasons. Sometimes it's because you're adopting an overly passive approach to a task; or, on the flip side, you're being so proactive that you can't settle on a decision. Let's say that this scale has 'analysis paralysis' on one end and 'passive approach' on the other.

On the more proactive end of the scale, analysis paralysis causes you to overthink a decision to the point where it is never made. This phenomenon often occurs when you fear that the end result won't meet your idea of the 'perfect solution'. In an investing context, you may be so scared that your analysis won't result in a great investment that you fail to follow through with a purchase. This leaves you with nothing but mountains of valid research and no properties to show for it. Analysis paralysis can also lead to decision fatigue, where a poor decision is made after an extended amount of decision-making time.

Let's look at an example of how this can happen. You might be researching a particular property in a well-performing suburb. You go and inspect the property and find it has excellent potential with all the in-demand characteristics for the suburb's demographic. The agent informs you that the seller is motivated and that they will keenly await your offer. Overall, the property and conditions sound fantastic. However, upon leaving the property you start to have second thoughts and begin to doubt your research. You allow inaction to take hold of your decision-making abilities without pausing to think about the diminishing returns of the investment. You start to worry that if you commit to this investment property and buy it, you'll suddenly find a gem on the market that you're not able to take up. All of these irrational thoughts begin to plague your research and undermine your active approach, causing you to miss out on the real opportunity that is in front of you.

On the other end of the scale, taking a passive approach to investing will also result in missing out. If you adopt an overly relaxed mindset in the property game and fail to take proactive and motivated measures, you will be beaten by buyers who are more prepared.

For example, imagine you're a listing agent. You have two potential buyers come through and inspect a property that you're selling on your vendor's behalf. One buyer seems like they're simply there for a casual look around. They ask a handful of questions regarding the property but fail to ask important questions such as the reason the vendor is selling and whether there's been much interest in the property so far.

The other potential buyer, however, appears motivated and well-researched. They inform you that they've been looking around the area for prospective investments, ask all of the right questions, and state that they will be submitting an offer. They also provide their mobile phone number and ask you to give them a call if there's any more information that you require. As an agent, you already start to paint a picture in your mind of which buyer you would prefer to work with. A proactive and well-researched buyer will be more likely help you and your vendor achieve a quick settlement than an unmotivated, unprepared buyer.

**Solution:** The solution to analysis paralysis and the passive approach are quite similar. Be proactive with your market research, and when it comes time to submit an offer or walk away from the property, do it. To be effective in your analysis, we recommend you create a list of all of the calculations you want to make once you find a suitable listing. Once you find an opportunity, calculate the rental yield and capital growth estimations for the property, find comparable sales to inform your negotiation strategy and ask for valuations or rental appraisals from nearby agents who know the area well.

Once you've completed all your research, submit your offer to the listing agent and remain available for follow-up calls. Taking a proactive approach and being available for follow-up discussions with the listing agent can be crucial to success, so ensure you're available after you've submitted your offer. Also ensure that you follow the correct procedures and complete all of the relevant paperwork as set out by the listing agent. This will minimise any lost time due to incomplete or incorrect administration. Like all people, listing agents are busy, and they will certainly appreciate proactive and motivated buyers who make the effort to follow procedures, are available for calls and fill out the paperwork correctly and on time!

If you know you're overly passive in your approach or consistently freeze when it comes to decision time, remember: the best time to invest was yesterday, but luckily the second-best time is today. The more days, weeks, months or years you decide to sit on your hands and wait for the perfect property, the more days in market you lose. This means lost growth and diminishing rental returns, which is the enemy of successful investing. Continue to stay motivated and engaged in the market and you'll greatly reduce your risk of missing out on properties. Set yourself apart from other prospective buyers to the agent. Agents want to work with motivated and engaged buyers, not buyers who lack preparedness and availability.

To summarise, here are our top tips for actively engaging with listing agents:

- Ask engaging and worthwhile questions during inspections (don't be a timewaster).

- If you keep missing out on properties, engage with agents across the region and express your interest. Ask about current market trends and strategies you can enact to make your offers more competitive.

- Utilise a proactive approach with listing agents. Be open and available for communication during the negotiation period and follow the correct procedures.

## CHALLENGES WITH FINANCING

Now that we've covered off the most common challenges when it comes to missing out on properties, we'll take a look at common financing issues for investors.

It's no secret that one of the biggest financing challenges is a lack of required borrowing capacity to enter desirable areas of the market. This can be frustrating, but if you fail to adapt to the market and maintain flexibility when it comes to your chosen suburbs, you'll simply run into the same challenges that were explained earlier and start to miss out on opportunities.

There are numerous contributing factors to your overall borrowing capacity provided by lenders. These include:

- your expenses and lifestyle costs
- your income source, including your salary and other income such as rental income
- your property deposit and any other genuine savings
- your credit history
- any existing debt against your name – this includes personal loans, credit cards and mortgages.

All of these factors can either increase or reduce your borrowing capacity. If you find yourself with a bad credit history, too much debt, countless expenses, exuberant lifestyle costs and a modest source of income, you may quickly find that your borrowing capacity is not as high as you initially estimated. This can greatly limit your price point for investing opportunities and the areas in Australia where you can comfortably invest.

**Solution:** There are many ways that you can take action to increase your borrowing capacity, but these actions will require adaptability. Firstly, you can lower your expenses and find areas where your budget can incorporate flexibility. This can be achieved through minimising subscriptions and reducing the amount of disposable income spent during the period that your lender will view your bank summaries. If lenders see that you're consistently spending discretional income on items such as food deliveries or online shopping orders, you run the risk that the lender will view these regular purchases as expenses, which will lower your overall monthly income and consequently your borrowing capacity. If you can enact adaptability and positive habits over the few months that lenders will analyse your bank statements for, you can greatly increase your borrowing capacity. Don't forget the aggregation of marginal gains that we covered earlier – the smallest of positive habits can result in big changes.

Secondly, you can take action and pay down your credit cards or, better yet, get rid of them entirely. Even if your credit card with a limit of $20,000 has never been used or has a balance owing of $0.00, lenders will still interpret this as $20,000 debt against your name, which can reduce your borrowing capacity by multiple times the limit of that credit card. This is because you, as the credit card holder, have the ability to max out that credit card whenever you please. This poses a significant risk to the lender and their trust in you as a customer to pay back your loans, hence the reduced borrowing capacity. If you can go without credit cards during your search for a property, you may want to consider paying down or cancelling these credit cards to minimise your expenses and maximise your monthly income to increase your borrowing capacity.

In addition to addressing your credit cards, consolidating and paying down any existing personal loans can also greatly enhance your borrowing capacity. To prioritise your debts, analyse which debt is incurring the highest interest rate. This should be the first loan you pay off, so you can save on interest. All debts after that can be prioritised in order from the most interest incurred to the least. With lower debts and repayments, you will likely be able to borrow more.

Thirdly, alternative lenders can also provide you with varying borrowing capacities. Every lender is different and will analyse your expenses via different methods. If you fail to achieve the borrowing capacity that you desired, you can investigate other lenders or ask your broker to investigate tier 2 or 3 lenders depending on your situation.

Tier 2 and 3 lenders differ to tier 1 banks in that they can be more flexible when it comes to their ability to grant loans. Tier 2 and 3 lenders have different policies: their staff can often utilise more judgement and discretion when viewing applications and can create an individual risk assessment per application. Tier 1 lenders, on the other hand, are more prone to utilising a strict and rigid process to assess all applications.

Overall, there are many ways that you can proactively enhance your borrowing capacity. All it takes is adaptability and flexibility within your personal finances. Again, a mortgage broker can be your trusted navigator in the world of lending. If you have doubts about how lenders are viewing your applications, we highly recommend that you find yourself a trusted broker to guide you through the process.

## CHALLENGES DURING THE ACQUISITION PROCESS

If you have already managed to break into the property market, you will know that the journey to settlement isn't always smooth sailing. The acquisition process can bring about its own challenges, which will require adaptability and flexibility to effectively close the deal.

Some of the biggest challenges can occur after the property's building and pest inspection is completed. For many deals, this inspection can be make or break, particularly if the property is an older established property.

Common issues that are uncovered by building and pest inspections include asbestos, presence of termites, broken appliances, movement in the property's structure, requirements for minor or major structural repairs, water damage and many more.

Once the inspector informs you of what the property needs, you should conduct your own research before you can make a decision on the property. How much will the repairs cost? Does the cost undermine the return that you've calculated for the property? Will it take a long time to repair, and if so, how much rental income will you lose in the interim? Is it worth your time? These are key questions that you will have to ask yourself and ensure you factor into the cost-benefit analysis for each property.

**Solution:** If you complete your due diligence and still think that the property is worth buying, ensure you factor the cost of the repairs into your negotiation strategy. You can do this by sourcing multiple quotes from different businesses for the work that needs to be completed, and then taking these quotes into negotiations with the agent. This illustrates to the agent that you've completed your due diligence and know how much the repairs will cost you as a buyer. It will illustrate to the agent that you're informed and motivated, and it will also help you to quickly complete the repairs prior to tenanting the property.

If the property's repair requirements reduce your expected return on investment, ensure that you walk away. Building and pest inspections are there to protect the buyer. If the juice isn't worth the squeeze, don't let decision fatigue warp your decision-making abilities. It will be frustrating to walk away from a property that you might have analysed and researched for a long time, but don't let the factor of time affect your ability to assess the pros and cons effectively.

### CHALLENGES DURING THE CONTRACT EXCHANGE PERIOD

You may also experience challenges during the contract exchange period. This is the period in which contracts for the property are exchanged between the vendor and the buyer, and the countdown to settlement is on. Challenges relating to pre-settlement inspection standards, building and pest inspection results, financing and special contract conditions can arise during this period. We're not saying that these problems will always arise (and we hope that you never have to experience challenges in the lead up to settlement!) but being aware of what can happen is important for your own preparation.

### Pre-settlement inspections

One of the challenges during this period can be the conducting of pre-settlement inspections. The pre-settlement inspection ensures that the property you receive is in a satisfactory condition. If the pre-settlement inspection isn't conducted to a high standard – or isn't conducted at all – you may incur additional cleaning or repair costs to get the property up to scratch. This can happen if you live interstate and don't have an opportunity to inspect the property yourself, having to rely on a property manager or real estate agent to do the inspection on your behalf.

**Solution:** Ensuring that the pre-settlement inspection is completed to an acceptable standard can help you avoid these problems. We recommend that if you have a property manager in the area that you intend to utilise for the property, you request that they conduct the inspection for you. Property managers are well-versed in conducting inspections and they know what to look for when it comes to pre-settlement. It also provides the property manager insight into the condition of the property before helping you find tenants to rent your new investment.

### Missed damage or required repairs

Even after the pre-settlement and building and pest inspections, the property may be left in an untidy state, and damage or necessary repairs may be overlooked. These problems can heavily impact special conditions in the property's contract such as 'property must be clean and free from rubbish' or 'all appliances and electrical items must be in working condition'. Although this is rare, especially if you engage a qualified and experienced property manager or building and pest inspector, it can happen. If you manage to pick up any problems during the exchange period, it may impact the contractual terms of the agreement and end up impacting the property's planned settlement date.

**Solution:** In this situation, you must alert the real estate agent and vendor's solicitor to the fact that the terms of the contract haven't been completed. If the property is untidy or there are faults with the property that result in a direct breach of one of your special clauses, you usually have four options to propose to the vendor. You can:

- ask that the vendor fixes the issues that currently breach the contract
- request that the seller pays you to fix the issues
- elect to delay settlement up until the time the vendor takes action to rectify the situation
- walk away from the deal.

Overall, these solutions will differ depending on your contract and the property that you're buying, but they're good strategies to know. Always ensure you conduct your research and engage in discussions with your solicitor if necessary.

### Finance falls through

Any problems regarding finance during the exchange process can be very daunting. Even with pre-approval, you may find yourself vulnerable to a range of finance-based challenges prior to settlement. These include receiving a low valuation from the lender that doesn't match the property's selling price, changes in personal circumstances affecting your borrowing capacity, or changes in the lender's policies affecting your loan.

**Solution:** Firstly, if your property valuation comes back lower than expected, you can either request to renegotiate the offer with the listing agent or vendor, pay for the difference yourself or walk away from the deal. All of these situations pose their own unique challenges and solutions, but being aware that valuations can deviate from the negotiated selling price is important.

Secondly, sometimes personal circumstances change during your deal and you may have to re-evaluate your offer or the purchase overall. Sometimes these situations are unavoidable but completing your due diligence and ensuring that your personal finances are in order prior to making the decision to purchase can help. Prior preparation in the property game is everything.

Lastly, being aware that lender policies can change is important, even if you feel like you are safe underneath your pre-approval umbrella. Lender policies and products can change over time, and although this may be a scary thought, it's simply an element of investing that you have to be wary of. This is where your experienced and knowledgeable mortgage broker comes into play. Brokers can help you navigate the world of lending, and if your loan product ends up falling through, they are in the best position to help you salvage your deal. So, ensure that they are kept informed at all stages of your purchasing process in case you ever need to lean on them for advice and expertise.

### Challenges post-settlement

Even after settlement, you still need to remain flexible and adaptable during your period of property ownership. Problems can and will arise when owning investment properties and, as a wise investor, you must anticipate these. It's crucial to be as prepared and informed as you can.

You should aim to be prepared for any situation – from big challenges such as poor market performance and natural disasters such as fire and floods, to smaller challenges such as accidental tenant damage or unexpected repairs.

**Solution:** Although we all hope that our properties perform well in the market, the property cycle and market trends will certainly have a role to play in the outcomes. As iterated in previous steps, it is important to remain dedicated and disciplined during the boom and slump phases of the market. Although your property may go through phases where it's not performing as expected, it's important to keep revising your strategy and plan your next steps forward in your plan to grow your portfolio.

As for natural disasters, make sure you conduct research on the area and purchase the necessary insurances for your investment. Conducting suburb research prior to purchase will help provide you with an indication as to whether the area has been historically prone to fires, floods, storms or high winds, which will assist you in deciding which policies may be a best fit for the property.

For tenant-caused damage, this is where your property managers are worth their weight in gold. If the tenant has caused damage or has clearly not taken care of the property, your property manager should alert you to the issue and help you achieve a resolution with the tenant. If the issue cannot be resolved without some form of mediation or legal assistance, your property manager will also be able to represent you and your interests. Landlord insurances can also help protect you in the circumstance that your expected rental income is impacted as a result of tenancy problems.

Overall, the number of opportunities and risks in property investing is countless. Regardless of your level of preparation, your time spent in the market will never fail to surprise you. An uninformed or inexperienced investor may choose to stress about the unknown, or simply avoid investing in property altogether because of a perceived lack of control. Rather than stressing or avoiding investing, we simply ask that you choose to be a wise investor and remain as informed as possible during your time in the market. By enacting flexibility and adaptability in as many areas of your portfolio as possible, you can remain vigilant throughout your own investing journey.

# Step 9:
# DEDICATION

Dedication involves consistent commitment to your mission and objective. In the military, unparalleled amounts of dedication are displayed by serving personnel. Military members are all too familiar with the sacrifices required to remain dedicated to service life - particularly in situations of monumental stress and extended time away from friends and family.

Step 1: Reveille

Step 2: Discipline

Step 3: Teamwork

Step 4: Professional mastery

Step 5: Excellence

Step 6: Mission analysis

Step 7: Courage

Step 8: Adaptability and flexibility

**Step 9: Dedication**

Step 10: Loyalty

## Step 9: Dedication

In this chapter, we'll explore the tools and habits that you can use and develop to remain dedicated to your goals while on your investment journey.

### DEDICATION TO KEEP BUILDING YOUR PORTFOLIO

Dedication to your investing journey is critical to achieving financial freedom. As discussed in Step 2 – Discipline, many Australians will attempt to grow a property portfolio with an end goal of supplementing their working wage by creating a passive income. Unfortunately, a majority of these investors will cease their pursuits before their portfolio grows large enough to provide a steady source of passive income.

Let's reconsider the statistics we looked at in Step 7 – Courage. There are over 2.2 million Australians who currently own an investment property. This indicates that roughly one in five Australians has invested in property. Of these, 71 per cent own one property and just 19 per cent own two properties. The remaining 10 per cent of property investors own three or more properties. So, what does this data highlight to us? It indicates that too many investors are failing to dedicate the time, money and effort required to accumulate enough assets to create an ever-expanding, scalable and sustainable property portfolio.

We've mentioned this in earlier chapters but it's important to readdress it – one investment property simply will not generate enough returns to provide you with that golden nest egg you may be working for, nor a substantial enough passive income to supplement your working wage. Unless you hit the jackpot and purchase a house in a suburb that will one day experience insurmountable growth in the high double-digit figures, you're more than likely going to need to acquire more than just one investment property to achieve your financial goals.

Although securing one investment property is a fantastic achievement for many, it's going to take a significant amount of dedication and focus to create and enact a strategic plan to help you continue to grow your portfolio into the future. In this chapter we'll provide you with the tools required to build your own strategic plan and stick to it to make it over the first-property hump.

## RE-ENGAGING THE MARKET – HOW TO MAKE IT OVER THE FIRST-PROPERTY HUMP

There are numerous avenues you can investigate to re-engage the property market after your first purchase. If you are already over the first-property hump, these steps still very much apply to you and your next acquisition – no matter what number purchase you are up to.

Let's face it – we are all guilty of putting our investing endeavours on the backburner every now and then. Life can simply get in the way of us hustling and prioritising our finances. There are a myriad of reasons you might take time off from investing – whether it's because work has been incredibly busy, you've committed to further study, you're starting a family or you've moved overseas for work.

In saying this, we still urge all of our clients to set some time aside, whether it be monthly or bi-annually, to reassess their financial goals and their current monetary situation. This regular check-in is important: it allows you to continuously perform assessments and re-assessments of where you can make improvements in your budget or portfolio to prepare for your next acquisition. Setting aside time for self-reflection and horizon-scanning is critical to finding investing opportunities within your internal and external circles. We'll expand on horizon-scanning later in the chapter; for now, let's take a look at five steps and self-reflection tools that will enable you to remain dedicated to your investing journey.

## Saving for your next deposit

One of the key financial components of property investing is ensuring that you have a deposit prepared for your next acquisition. In most cases, you will need 10 per cent of the property's purchase price, plus closing costs and lenders mortgage insurance (if this isn't capitalised into the loan).

Saving for your next deposit may take some time, especially if you've recently purchased a property. However, this is when it is critical to assess your personal finances and spending habits. We recommend that all investors take a critical view of their income and expenses to see where adjustments can be made. Have you minimised the amount you need to spend on personal subscriptions? Are you spending a disproportionate amount of discretionary income rather than redirecting more of that income into your savings account?

Once you've identified the adjustments you can make to your personal finances, you can begin building a savings plan. This plan will also help you estimate the month and year that you'll be ready to begin your search for your next property. In the lead up, it's still important to conduct your own market research in order to analyse trends and begin narrowing down where you may want to buy your next investment.

## Exploiting equity

The next step you can take in preparation for your next purchase involves evaluating your current portfolio to search for any unused (or under-utilised) equity. Equity is simply the difference between the value of a property and any loans secured against it. Your equity will consist of the deposit you initially paid to buy the house, plus any market growth since your purchase and, finally, any of the mortgage that you've managed to pay off.

For example, a property that's been purchased for $500,000 with a loan of $400,000 has total equity of $100,000. If that property were to experience 5 per cent growth over the first year, then the property's equity would be $125,000 – since $25,000 was accumulated in growth (not including any mortgage repayments made over that year).

So, as your property's value rises over time, so will your equity. Even if you haven't made significant progress towards paying down the property's mortgage, useable equity will still increase as long as the property experiences growth. Adding improvements to the property, such as renovations, subdividing or other changes, can also add additional value to the house that will enhance the property's equity.

Once assessed, equity in a property can be utilised as a deposit on an additional property for your portfolio. In this scenario, the existing property acts as a security on the new debt for the lender. Your lender will calculate your property's LVR and hold onto some of the equity as security. Once that has occurred, you can evaluate how much residual equity can be utilised as a deposit for another property. Remember that additional funds will still be required for other costs including stamp duty and legal fees.

### Revisiting your strategic plan

After purchasing a property, it's important to revisit your strategic plan and the end goal for your portfolio. In Step 2 – Discipline, we explained the three levels of military planning: tactical, operational and strategic. If you're between purchases, this means that you've successfully purchased your first property, and it aligned with your overall strategic plan – that is, purchasing a property that generates high cash flow, capital growth or both. But now that you've reached that first milestone, it's important to reflect on your strategy and take time to plan your next step – and what better time to do that than post-purchase, when you're between acquisitions?

Let's take a look at an example. Ben's strategic goal for his financial future is to create a balanced portfolio of properties that generates both excellent cash flow and capital growth. A year ago, he purchased his first property – a negatively geared residential property in a blue-chip suburb in Melbourne. The property has grown over 7 per cent in the past year, which is on track with Ben's goal for a high-growth acquisition. The suburb is highly desirable to tenants thanks to its location and features, and Ben is able to comfortably cover the gap between the property's rental income and mortgage repayments from his own pocket.

After taking a year to save for his next deposit, Ben is now on the hunt for his next acquisition. Before conducting his market research, Ben takes some time to consult his broader strategy and begin planning his next property. Since Ben was able to successfully purchase a high-growth property that satisfies the capital gains component of his portfolio, he decides to begin searching for properties that can provide high rental yields to satisfy the other side of his balanced strategy. A property that generates high cash flow will also help Ben, so he doesn't have to continue paying any more money out of his pocket for a second negatively geared property.

As we can see from Ben's example, evaluating your strategy can help you identify what your portfolio needs to make it stronger. Taking some time to reflect on your wider strategy may seem simple, but remember that the simplest parts of a plan can be the easiest to forget! After your first property purchase, you can gain a lot of confidence and begin to think about all of the other avenues through which you can invest your money. Taking time to sit down and consult your original plan will help remind you of your goal at the end of the journey. Overall, plans and end states can change, but remember to do your research and calculations so you can ensure that the properties you purchase will help you get there!

### Setting smart goals

You may already be familiar with the concept of setting SMART goals. These goals, when implemented in a property-investing context, can enable you to evaluate your current financial situation and desired end state through assessing five key components:

- **Specific:** Your goal needs to be specific so you can maintain your focus and energy on the desired end state. A specific goal does not sound like: 'I want to accumulate property so I can live financially free.' A specific goal *does* sound like: 'I will aim to purchase one property every two years in order to achieve $80,000 passive income to replace my annual wage to spend more time with my family.'

- **Measurable:** Your goal must also be measurable in order for you to track your progress and stay motivated. Progress can be found in many areas of property investing – not just on the days when you settle on a new property. Progress looks like your property increasing in value over the past year. Progress looks like sticking to your financial budget so you can continue saving for your next deposit. As long as your goals are measurable and provide you with identifiable progress milestones, you will be able to keep yourself more accountable to your investing journey.

- **Achievable:** We're all guilty of setting unachievable goals at various points in our lives. Perhaps you want to lose 5 kg in one week before a big social event, or save $50,000 in one year when you know that you've only been able to achieve savings of $20,000 in previous years. Goals need to be realistic and within your reach, while encouraging you to strive and push your boundaries. If you don't set realistic and achievable goals, you're purposefully setting yourself up for failure and disappointment. This will cause you to feel deflated and unmotivated – two feelings that have no place in the fast-paced world of the property game. We encourage you to take a step back and set yourself an achievable, overarching goal, and then start setting up micro-goals to track your progress along the way.

- **Relevant/realistic:** Ensuring that your goals are relevant to your end state will help you categorise and prioritise your objectives. For example, getting a promotion and subsequent pay rise at work may help you advance both your career and your investment goals. While planning out your goals for property investing, ensure that you evaluate your other goals for yourself and your family so you can map out any interrelated goals. It is also important to make sure that your goals are realistic. Although we're sure that many people have dreamed about owning a $100 million property portfolio, a more realistic goal might be to aim for a $5 million portfolio to start with. This will help you stay motivated and enable you to align the areas of effort and energy.

- **Time-bound:** This is a key area where we find many investors fall down. Let's look back at the statistic that shows us that only 29 per cent of Australian property investors make it over the first-property hump. You can rest assured that the investors who own two or more properties had a time-bound investment plan that enabled them to remain focused and motivated on their portfolio-building journey. Goals are nothing without timelines. Having a set time in mind helps you prepare for your next acquisition and will help you identify time periods where you need to reassess your current portfolio and budget. In the military, without timelines, missions quickly fall apart. Objectives are missed and important information is either neglected or rendered inaccurate. The property market is no different. Understand when you intend to take action and purchase your next property so you can arm yourself with current market information, a secured source of finance and an objective.

### Alternative routes to keep growing your portfolio

Most property investors will reach a time in the acquisition phase of their portfolio where there's simply nothing to do but wait. After purchasing your first, second or third property, you may find yourself either maxed out of borrowing capacity or with no spare cash left for deposits. Understand that this is totally fine and completely normal. After our third property purchase, we even found ourselves hitting a wall. We thought to ourselves, 'We want to keep growing, but we've done all we can. We've got next to no borrowing capacity or spare cash left – so what now?'

This can be a frustrating part of the acquisition process, but shouldn't leave you unmotivated. Sometimes there's nothing more you can do in your situation than wait to grow another deposit for your next purchase or wait for your properties to increase in value to provide you with enough equity to re-engage with the market.

For those who can't wait and need to keep busy with their portfolios, there are some other options outside of buying more properties. The first option is improvements. Improvements and renovations do require some money, but they are a good option if you find yourself with some left-over cash but no borrowing capacity to purchase another property. Improvements can include landscaping, painting, room remodels, installation of fans or air conditioning and more. Not all improvements have to be incredibly expensive. If you happen to live in the same area as your investment property, you might even be able to implement some improvements yourself. For more substantial improvements that require trades expertise, always remember to source quotes from three or more businesses in order to attain the best value for money without compromising on quality.

If you have cash in your pockets, you may also opt to develop a granny flat to enhance your property's value. As we learned in Step 5 – Excellence, granny flats can provide a low-cost, high-return investment. While boosting the amount of liveable space on the property for tenants, granny flats can enhance the rental yield and overall value of the property. Although they are a great option for many, investors should remain aware that they may not be appropriate for all dwellings and the plans will often require council approval prior to building.

If you want to sink your teeth into an even larger project, subdividing and splitting can also be a very profitable option. Subdivision is when a property owner requests that the council divide an existing block into two (which can be differently sized). You will require a planning permit to subdivide and should conduct all of your research and budgeting to ensure the subdivision will result in a profitable outcome. Considerations such as minimum lot size, minimum frontage size and council zoning will also be imperative as to whether or not you can subdivide your property.

As we learned in Step 5 – Excellence, splitting a block is different to subdivision in that splitter blocks typically consist of two lots that are on a single land title. Splitter blocks are commonly seen in many areas such as Brisbane, where an existing house typically straddles the two lots of land. In order to effectively split the block, the existing property may need to be demolished to make room for two individual properties – one for each lot.

If you shy away from getting your hands dirty with subdivision, splitting and improvements but want to hop back into the property game quickly, there are other avenues available. Joint ventures, syndicates and partnerships enable you to join arms with other avid investors who may not have the cash or borrowing capacity required to invest solo, but do have enough funds to enter a collaborative venture.

Syndicate groups, partnerships and joint ventures account for the general practice of two or more investors banding their finances together in order to develop or purchase property. Profits generated by the development or established property are then split between the investors according to the agreement that each party enters.

Some property development businesses even specialise in the formal arrangement of syndicate groups. Investors will come to the business with their available finance and the business will take on the responsibility of arranging the finances of the syndicate members and investing into a trust account that pays for a preconceptualised development. After the properties sell, the developer then takes a cut of the profits and divides the rest among the investors.

To recap, there are five effective tools that you can utilise to remain dedicated to your property-investing journey during times when you're not actively in the market:

1. continue to save for your next deposit
2. exploit equity
3. establish or revisit your strategic plan
4. set your SMART goals
5. explore and evaluate alternate routes.

Now that we've covered how you can stay active in the property game while waiting on the sidelines, we're going to take a deep dive into several other activities that are key to maintaining and scaling your existing investment portfolio. Even if you're not looking at purchasing in the near future, maintaining the health and trajectory of your existing portfolio is still key to ensuring future success.

## CONDUCTING PORTFOLIO DILIGENCE

Taking stock can help you keep track of your progress in relation to your goals. This is where portfolio diligence can come in handy.

An important component of portfolio diligence is the re-evaluation of your income, mortgage, loans, rental income and personal budget to see what can be improved on and maximised in order to achieve your goals sooner.

You can't always secure that pay rise or promotion that could help you supercharge the inflow of cash into your household, but you can take control of the money that flows out of your household. If you're like most Australian families, your largest expense will be your mortgage. It is therefore crucial that you ensure that you're conducting market research to secure the best-going interest rate. If you do some research and see that there are other lenders that are offering better deals, take the time to analyse whether refinancing could be an option for you.

To illustrate the benefits of refinancing, let's look at two home loans for the same house (table 9.1). Let's say that a house was purchased for $500,000 and a 10 per cent deposit was paid upon settlement. The remaining $450,000 was financed with a principal and interest loan at a rate of 3.5 per cent per annum for a period of 30 years. This totals to a monthly repayment of $2,020.70. Let's say that the owner decided to shop around to find a better rate. They found a lender offering a principal and interest loan of 3 per cent per annum. With this rate, the monthly repayments drop to $1,897.22. Over the 30 years, a 0.5 per cent difference in the interest rate totals a substantial saving of $44,453.

### Table 9.1: Example home loan savings

| Principal and interest loan at 3.5% | | Principal and interest loan at 3.0% | |
|---|---|---|---|
| Principal: | $450,000 | Principal: | $450,000 |
| Interest rate: | 3.5% | Interest rate: | 3.0% |
| Monthly repayment: | $2,020.70 | Monthly repayment: | $1,897.22 |
| Repayment difference: | +$123.48 | Repayment difference: | -$123.48 |
| Savings from refinancing over 30 years: | | | $44,453 |

Of course, interest rates will rise and fall over the years, but this example illustrates the power of shopping around and conducting due diligence when it comes to one of your household's largest expenses.

Keeping your finger on the pulse of your surrounding market can be critical when it comes time to refinance your home loan. If you attempt to refinance when your local market is entering a downturn phase of the property cycle, your lender could come back with a lower valuation for your home than when you purchased – which would cause you to lose equity. But if you choose to refinance your loan at a time when your local market is entering an upturn or boom, a lender will hopefully come back with a more favourable value for your home. This will arm you with additional equity that you can use for your next investment. As an additional bonus, refinancing may provide you with the opportunity to switch to a loan with lower interest (depending on the interest-rate environment).

The second key point for portfolio diligence lies with your investment properties. Not only should you be maintaining an interest in the suburb that your own home is situated in, you should also be monitoring the suburbs that your investments are situated in. This will help you when it comes time to make key decisions such as raising the rent, refinancing to pull out useable equity or selling the property. Tenants are protected by law when it comes to raising the rent in abrupt and considerable amounts, so ensure that rents are raised incrementally and in line with the market. This is where periodic market analysis and horizon-scanning can come in handy.

Horizon-scanning is an analytical tool commonly used when the military looks to acquire new and emerging technologies, systems or weaponry. Horizon-scanning provides the military with foresight rather than hindsight when it comes to assessing future opportunities and threats. As an investor, your horizon-scanning can come in the form of suburb analysis, market-trend analysis, or engaging with your expert team members so they can notify you of upcoming market opportunities or potential pitfalls. This enables you to remain engaged and alert in the property game.

Investors who choose not to remain diligent or engage in periodic horizon-scans will most likely find themselves out of the loop when it comes to critical market indicators. These investors will fail to raise rents when their suburb is in demand with prospective tenants, and may even miss an opportune time to sell if the area experiences a considerable double-digit growth boom. These poor inattentive investors will eventually miss out on thousands of dollars of rental income and capital returns. Never forget that the basics of property investing are easy in principle but will always take diligence, discipline, dedication and effort to implement.

## METHODS OF LONG-TERM EDUCATION

If you've performed all of the re-engagement preparation and portfolio diligence you can do, taking a break to educate yourself can be incredibly advantageous for yourself, your properties and your investing future.

Taking the time to reflect after an acquisition can be a great way to expand your education base and capture lessons learned. During this self-reflection, it may be opportune to ask yourself:

- How did that acquisition go?
- What would I have done differently if I could go back again?
- Does this acquisition bring me closer to my goals?
- Which areas can I research better for next time?

In the military, taking time to reset after a mission and dedicate time to personal development is key for all units. This period is critical for relaxation after a long time spent away from family and friends, or after a particularly challenging exercise or operation.

Capturing lessons learned is also prioritised so that future missions can benefit from learning the history of those who have gone before them. Scheduling personnel onto professional development courses during this time ensures that members can continue growing their knowledge base as they take a break from the implementation side of their professions.

As property investors, we recommend that you also set time aside after each purchase to capture key lessons learned throughout the acquisition process and dedicate time to personal development and education.

If you don't necessarily want to go spending considerable amounts of money on formal education, there are plenty of accessible educational resources out there. Some of these include state associations such as Real Estate Institutions, TAFE, universities and online learning providers. Other sources include online data repositories, blogs, forums and books (like this one!).

Also be on the lookout for property-related seminars and presentations. These seminars can be hosted and attended by like-minded investors who may be able to offer great advice from personal experience. Conferences are often hosted by property associations or private businesses that specialise in selling developments, or financial advising services that specialise in the property realm.

Like all things in life, be aware that seminars run by private businesses may have an agenda for their intended audience. Seminars hosted by private businesses will most likely contain biased statistics and information, because they probably want to upsell you on their products or services. If you commit to attending these seminars, we recommend that you attend with pre-established boundaries, such as, 'I won't sign up to anything on the day. I will go away and think about the services before signing up.' Overall, property-related seminars can be a fantastic way to broaden your education base, network with industry experts, and even make some like-minded friends along the way.

If you decide you want to undertake formal tertiary or vocational studies, there are multiple certificates, diplomas, online courses and university subjects available. Courses range across a variety of topics, including property valuation, portfolio planning, property investment and appraisal, data analysis, property law, urban planning, architectural and interior design, and more. No matter what area of property you're interested in, there are formal educational subjects out there for you. We recommend identifying an area that you're most interested to study so you can remain motivated and engaged in the property game. There are always experts out there that can help you in the areas that you're not so confident in!

## A PATH FORWARD

As an investor, it's likely you will face a strong sense of frustration once you have reached the limit of your borrowing capacity for investment purposes. We've provided you with a broad range of activities that can be conducted in the interim until you're financially prepared to re-engage in the property market. However, one of the key things that you must do as a dedicated investor is remain focused on your end goal – securing financial freedom. The idle times are the riskiest for inexperienced investors. Some investors simply don't want to sit still, so they search for another investing lane that they can explore in the interim while they wait until they can purchase their next property. This enthusiasm is fantastic and should be utilised, but in ways that will advance your investing journey – not hinder or delay the realisation of your end goal even further.

We have seen too many investors take risks and lose money in short-term investments because they didn't want to enact patience and dedication throughout their journey. Instead of growing their savings and taking the time to research and plan for their next investment, they go and inject their money into high-risk, short-term investments in hope that they can make some quick cash. These actions demonstrate an effect called 'mission creep', which we will explore in greater detail in Step 10 – Loyalty.

Shifting objectives and diverting attention away from your primary goal can often be a negative and counteractive path to wander down. We recommend occupying yourself with the productive activities that we have just talked about so you can stay focused on your primary objective.

# Step 10:
# LOYALTY

Loyalty to your mates, mission and personal development is instilled within all serving military personnel. Both the training and operational environments are specifically designed to encourage members to discard their individual differences and unite as a coherent and fiercely loyal team. The bond formed between soldiers, sailors, airmen and airwomen and their teams is a bond like no other.

Step 1: Reveille

Step 2: Discipline

Step 3: Teamwork

Step 4: Professional mastery

Step 5: Excellence

Step 6: Mission analysis

Step 7: Courage

Step 8: Adaptability and flexibility

Step 9: Dedication

**Step 10: Loyalty**

# Step 10: Loyalty

Through shared experience, fear, triumph and hardship, serving personnel form a sense of loyalty to their fellow team members that is incomparable to any other relationship. Whether it be overseas, in the training environment or at home, military members remain united no matter how much time passes.

## LOYALTY TO YOURSELF, YOUR TEAM AND YOUR GOAL

By this point we can all agree that property investing is a strategic, long-term commitment. It's no secret that achieving financial freedom through property will take many years, numerous acquisitions, periods of frustration, and patience during the time in between. To remain committed to your desired financial end state, loyalty to yourself, your team and your goal will certainly be required.

Firstly, loyalty to your team will be absolutely critical on your property journey. In the deployed environment, military personnel are taught to trust their team members and their specific areas of expertise. A ship's captain will unwaveringly trust their chief engineer's training and expertise to ensure a ship keeps running during a tactical transit of a body of water, and an intelligence officer will consistently maintain confidence in their fellow analysts' assessments. That's because military relationships are built upon a basis of mutual trust and respect of each other's training and experiences.

The business and property-investment world is no different. Thanks to the ever-growing accessibility of information and education, we are certainly living in a 'do it yourself' era. These days, we can easily search for an investment loan through a plethora of comparison websites, and we can also scroll through the 250,000 to 350,000 properties that are listed for sale every single year in Australia.

Access to these tools enables you as an investor to educate yourself and grow your personal knowledge base about property and the overall industry, without the assistance of industry professionals. However, we suggest and highly encourage you to place your trust in the experts, such as mortgage brokers, solicitors, buyer's agents (BAs) and other professionals, to help you achieve your property goals.

One of the main reasons we recommend trusting industry experts is because we understand that we can't all be experts in every single area of life, particularly in property and investing. Property investing lies at a unique nexus of a wide variety of industries. These include law, finance, construction, development, management, real estate and more. If you analyse the property industry with a critical lens, you will quickly realise that you'll rarely find a mortgage broker who doubles as a conveyancer, or a builder who works as a sales agent on weekends. This is because all of these experts understand and respect their professional limitations and are willing to trust other industry experts to assist them in areas where they aren't well practised. We recommend that you do the same.

During our years of investing for ourselves and our clients, we have repeatedly witnessed investors making the following common mistakes:

- trusting a friend to conduct a building and pest inspection for their property
- asking a family member to help them find a great tenant with excellent tenancy history
- deciding to source their own investment loan rather than utilising the skills of an experienced mortgage broker
- and many, many more!

We've observed just about every single scenario you can think of, and all too often these shortcuts result in a negative outcome: the bank is late delivering finance to the buyer because the loan paperwork was not correctly submitted; the building inspector missed a crucial structural issue; or the family friend doesn't find a suitable tenant in a timely fashion, which resulted in lost rental income (just to name a few). Figure 10.1 illustrates a range of other risks that you take on if you don't utilise the skills of professionals. These risks can quickly turn into substantial issues that can negatively impact the settlement process for a property.

*Figure 10.1: Common mistakes that put your settlement at risk*

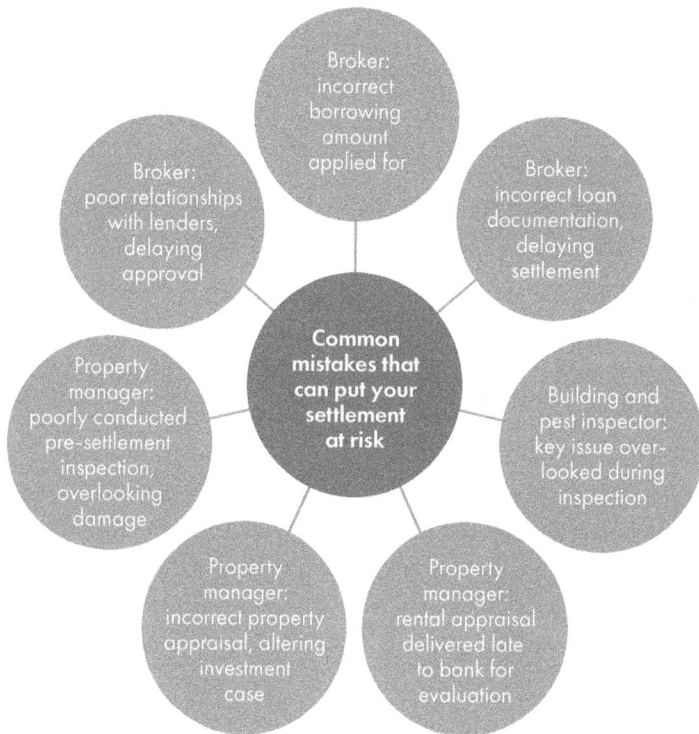

So, what's the lesson we want you to take away from this? You need to trust the experienced experts and remain loyal to your trusted team. It's simply not worth seeing a fantastic market deal fall through the cracks because you wanted to save a few thousand dollars by doing it yourself or trusting an unqualified friend who's promised to give you mates rates. The number of excellent property sales that we have seen fail because the buyer wasn't appropriately prepared or chose to trust a sub-par professional is far higher than we'd care to admit. We strongly suggest that you maintain a future-based perspective and invest your time, money and peace of mind in someone whose day job and reputation relies on them delivering a professional and trustworthy service.

### You get what you pay for – always

Like everything in life, you always get what you pay for. If you choose to pay for quality the first time, chances are you'll only ever have to pay once.

As we mentioned before, it is natural to want to 'shop around' to find quality service at a reasonable price. However, we want to highlight the stark difference between shopping around and due diligence when it comes to finding quality business partners to work with. The best accountant, pest and building inspector, property manager or solicitor for your purchase will not always be the cheapest provider on the market.

Rather than shopping around to find the professional with the lowest going rate, ensure that you conduct your due diligence on the professional. Learn about their qualifications and experience in the market while picturing yourself doing business with them in the future. As long as their services are fairly priced, we recommend utilising them if everything else stacks up – even if they're not the cheapest option you can find. You want to be able to trust the professional's experience and opinion and be comfortable calling them for urgent business. You may find yourself paying slightly more for their services, but you will also be paying for additional peace of mind in future dealings.

This is where we link loyalty in. Once you've found your perfect team member who is professional, experienced and well-versed in their area of industry, we recommend that you stick by them for the long-haul and continue to build a solid relationship with them. Relationship-building in any industry is crucial, but even more so in property investing. Property deals will always be associated with high costs and time crunches to get loan paperwork submitted, inspections completed and potential tenants through the door. Every investor should strive for a streamlined process, because in this game, time is money. If you find an industry professional who's worth their salt, they'll respect your time and do everything they can to complete their part of the deal so you can rest easy.

As buyer's agents (BAs), we reap the benefits of our professional relationships every single day. Most of our clients' property purchases are sourced pre-market or off-market. These pre-market and off-market purchases always have a time-critical element associated with them, primarily because the vendor wants a swift or private sale. But any time delays in creating and submitting an offer to the vendor can quickly cause issues. Time delays can be caused by things like receiving a late rental appraisal from a property manager, or a delayed response from the bank because a broker did not submit the loan documents on time. These delays can cause a vendor to change their mind and go ahead with commencing public inspections for their property. This usually means there will be an influx of competing offers from other prospective buyers and a loss of exclusivity over the listing for our clients.

This example demonstrates the importance of swift and decisive action when it comes to making a move on a listing. If your team members aren't prepared and working hard for you, you can quickly lose exclusivity over a quality investment-grade property. Sticking to your timings and ensuring that you work with a sense of urgency when you're in the market can be the difference between securing excellent properties or missing out every time.

## LOYALTY TO YOUR MISSION

During your property-investing journey, there will be times when you will feel like you want to stray away from your end goal of financial freedom and pursue a different venture. You might decide you want to purchase a brand-new home for yourself and your family because you're tired of renting, or perhaps you want to invest some cash in shares because your next deposit goal feels so far away. No matter where you want to put your money, ensure that you consider the action and how it fits with your strategic goal. Ask yourself, 'Will this action actually help me achieve my goal in the long run, or is it simply a distraction?' If the action will assist you in the long run and you've played out all of the possible scenarios, then go for it. But if you critically analyse the decision and realise that it will distract you from achieving your overall end state, you have to forget about it and refocus.

### Mission creep

The military term 'mission creep' helps us conceptualise this incremental drift from our original goals. Mission creep, as illustrated in figure 10.2, describes the gradual movement or expansion of a mission's initial scope and objectives. We wanted to address this concept in this chapter because the risk of mission creep is at its highest after an individual or team has achieved initial success in their operations. In this case, the risk of mission creep is at its highest after an investor has acquired their first investment property, or a seasoned investor has successfully added another property to their portfolio. Being aware of the consequences of mission creep can help you as an investor to ensure that you remain loyal and dedicated to your mission and your personal objectives while on your investing journey.

Success in itself brings confidence and a sense of achievement – it proves that the plan that you initially laid out for yourself is actually working! However, success might also give you cause to shift your gaze towards *what else* can be achieved. It's only natural that you are constantly looking towards other tasks that can be conquered so that you can continue to grow and personally develop.

*Figure 10.2: Mission creep*

Sticking to your
SMART goals and
investing timeline

Investing in asset classes
that don't align with your
original strategy

**Original mission scope** ⟶ **Mission creep**

Investing in properties
and other assets that align
with your strategy

Utilising your budget and
instilling financial habits that
further your goals

Missing key milestones
on your timeline

Adopting unnecessary
levels of risk

Purchasing out-of-budget
assets/properties

In Step 9 – Dedication, we discussed that there comes a time when you've done all you can with your available funds, and all that's left to do is sit tight until you accumulate enough funds or equity to make your next purchase. During times like these, it is easy to get distracted by other financial pursuits with lower barriers to entry or higher reward for 'slightly more risk', such as shares. During these times, remain loyal and diligent to your strategic plan and your desired end state. Continue to grow your savings, educate yourself and consistently review your goals and end state so you can remind yourself of your original mission. Remain loyal to the habits that enabled you to achieve success in the first place.

## STAY CURRENT WITH YOUR RESEARCH

Media commentary on property will always be painted with an extremely positive or negative light. Think about how many papers or online articles would be purchased if the finance section posted headlines announcing, 'National property market is doing okay!' This wouldn't sell nearly as many copies as articles titled, 'Property holders set to lose double-digit growth during COVID-19 pandemic', or 'Investors to reap highest quarter of growth on record.' The key lesson here? Pick your investing strategy and stick to it regardless of the surrounding commentary. Choose to conduct your research using reputable sources and remain loyal to your strategy.

Conducting your research will ensure that you're buying property at the most advantageous time in the property cycle. As covered earlier, there are over 15,000 suburbs in Australia and every single one of them is currently sitting at its own unique stage of its own individual property cycle. Just because a suburb was growing at 20 per cent per annum three years ago does not necessarily mean that the suburb is still experiencing excellent growth and is still in a boom phase today. In fact, it's more likely to be entering a downturn on its way to the bottom of the property cycle before increasing in demand again. Always ensure your research is current and that you conduct your research across a variety of sources and platforms.

## REMAIN LOYAL TO YOUR STRATEGY

Maintaining your strategic outlook and resisting mission creep can assist you in formulating a well-established portfolio that achieves your outcomes. For example, let's say you choose to enact a capital growth strategy for your overall portfolio. If you fail to conduct your market research or actively choose to stray from your overall strategy, you may accidentally purchase a property with excellent rental yields, but very low capital growth in a sub-par-performing suburb. This can quickly derail your portfolio's overarching strategy for capital growth.

Let's review the common property-investing strategies for typical Australians (table 10.1).

Table 10.1: Property-investing strategies

| Property strategy | Outcome | Suitable investor type |
| --- | --- | --- |
| Buy and hold | Capital growth | Passive investor |
| Renovation | Capital growth | Semi-active investor |
| Flipping | Capital growth | Active investor |
| Cash cow | Cash flow | Passive investor |
| Secondary dwelling | Cash flow | Semi-active investor |
| Development:<br>• Subdivision<br>• Splitting<br>• Knock down and rebuild<br>• Knock down and build (<$5 million)<br>• Knock down and build (>$5 million) | Capital growth | Active investor |

The property strategies listed can be achieved by any investor utilising a wide variety of asset types. These include established property, new (off-the-plan) property and even commercial property. Sticking to a certain dwelling type or condition (for example, new properties, apartments, established properties or commercial properties) isn't necessarily a strategy – it's a means to an end. It's simply a method of implementation to achieve a broader outcome for your portfolio.

## RIDE THE HIGHS AND LOWS OF THE PROPERTY CYCLE

Remaining dedicated and loyal to your investing journey won't always come easy. As covered in Step 4 – Professional mastery, the property cycle is an unavoidable element of all property investing, and it all comes down to the principle of supply versus demand.

Whenever there is a shortage of supply within an area, a rising and then peaking market should occur. This naturally causes an increase in price for the remaining stock. Although the peaking period is the phase of the cycle that all investors want their properties to experience, it's often the shortest-lived period of the entire property process. While prices can surge as high as 20 per cent or more during a peaking market, you mustn't feel discouraged when they inevitably experience a long slump period after a boom.

Slump phases are a predictable and natural consequence that you should prepare for if your property's suburb ever experiences a peaking period. Thanks to an extended period of high demand from buyers, the area is more likely to experience phases of over-development by builders and developers who are hoping to take advantage of the high prices that buyers are willing to pay. These developments create a significant influx of supply, which then extends the subsequent decline and slump periods post-boom.

During the slump phase of the cycle, you're likely to see an increase in vacancy rates. Unlike a peaking market, where the vendor or the landlord is in control, the buyer and the tenant have the buying and renting power. They have the pick of the litter, so to speak, when it comes to searching for properties to buy or rent on the market.

We're not highlighting the correlation between great booms and significant slumps to discourage you from holding onto property during the harder parts of the cycle. There are still excellent capital growth benefits that can be reaped from holding onto a property as it cycles through a peak phase. We simply want to emphasise the importance of remaining loyal to your property and your portfolio strategy during the more difficult and discouraging slump phases.

In our time, we've witnessed many investors sit back and happily observe their property entering a peak phase after the suburb experienced a downturn. Many buyers have been able to snag a bargain when the suburb was near the bottom of its property cycle – an opportune time to find a property, especially if there's a motivated seller. Despite knowing that property enters cycles of boom and decline, some investors simply aren't able to critically examine the market and trust that the suburb will bounce back.

This results in investors making rash and emotional decisions. They suddenly forget that the property is entering a natural part of its cycle because they see prices begin to fall, vacancy rates increase and buyer demand decline. Rather than critically analysing the situation and realising that the suburb is simply entering a rebalancing phase of supply and demand, they get scared and decide to sell the property.

In Step 4 – Professional mastery, we talked about how an investor is likely to have their property take between nine and 11 years to complete one full property cycle. So, if an investor gets scared off by a downturn phase after purchasing a property, it's likely that they haven't even held the property for more than a few years. If this is the case, the investor is also likely selling the property before it has experienced enough growth from the boom phase to cover their acquisition and selling costs, such as stamp duty, advertising, repairs or solicitor fees.

This example demonstrates the importance of remaining loyal to your strategy and holding onto your property during the peak and slump phases. There will always be opportune times in the property cycle to sell, but selling a property when the suburb is at the bottom of its cycle is never a productive way to reap your capital gains. A buy-and-hold strategy strongly relies on you buying and selling at opportune times, so ensure that your decision to enter and exit the market is based on analytical rigour and research rather than fear.

The lesson from this? Remain loyal to your property, portfolio and overarching strategy. You must understand that the boom periods will come and go, but so will the downturns. Trust the process, trust your team and trust your strategy! This will enable you and your family to commence your path to financial freedom.

# Final thoughts
## TAKING YOUR LEAVE

Committing yourself to personal education and development is a crucial first step on your investment journey. In the Navy, the term Bravo Zulu (BZ) is a common phrase meaning 'well done' and 'great work', and we want to say BZ to you for adding this book to your personal investment library. We hope that you've taken the time to highlight key points, scribble notes and write your own thoughts and experiences in the margins of these pages. Knowledge is absolutely key in the property game and we hope that you continue to commit yourself to personal education throughout your property journey.

We hope that you're able to enter or re-enter the investment world armed with more knowledge and confidence than what you had prior to finishing this book. Our goal in writing this book was to provide you with some sage advice and key lessons learned so you can avoid common pitfalls in property investing and succeed in your next acquisition.

Remember that every investment experience will be unique but will always hold true to the fundamentals of investing. As long as you remain dedicated and loyal to your goals, and keep the basics of successful investing in the forefront of your mind, you will achieve victory on your investing journey.

No matter your background or current financial situation, there are always ways that you can take control of your financial future. Any action, no matter how big or small, will help you achieve your own version of financial freedom. Whether you use property as your vehicle to generate enough passive income for an annual holiday, or enough cash to supplement your entire working wage, you are well on your way to achieving more than what your day job, superannuation or government pension could ever provide you with. Marginal gains, no matter how big or small, can result in monumental outcomes.

Remember to reap the rewards of your hard work. Staying dedicated to a financial goal is challenging and will require sacrifices, but remember that life is meant to be lived and enjoyed. Take your leave and remember to celebrate your achievements. Property will always be a means to an end, not the other way around. When the hard work is done, we hope that you can be proud of what you've accomplished and continue to inspire your family and friends around you.

We wish you all the very best on your investing journey.

## Buying an investment property
# A SIMPLIFIED CHECKLIST

If you haven't experienced the purchasing process before, buying an investment property can seem like a daunting prospect! We've broken it down into an easy-to-follow checklist so you can familiarise yourself with the basics before diving into the world of property ownership.

Remember that every purchase will be different and the order of these steps may vary. We recommend that you engage trusted industry professionals for their advice along the way.

☐ Devise your investment strategy and ask yourself whether you should be purchasing a property that will generate high cash flow, capital growth or a balance of both.

☐ Decide on your dwelling type: are you looking for a house, apartment, townhouse or land?

☐ Decide what your search criteria will include. Do you want a property with renovation potential? Subdivision or splitting potential? Room in the backyard for a granny flat?

☐ Decide on how you will finance the property. This includes arranging your pre-approval for a loan, gathering your deposit and determining what your borrowing capacity will be. This will help you search for properties that you can afford. This is the perfect time to engage with a mortgage broker so you can maximise your borrowing capacity, and therefore your budget!

☐ Once you've decided on your strategy, dwelling type, criteria and budget, it's time to commence your suburb research. What suburbs are demonstrating excellent micro factors for investing? Does the suburb have large sets of data available to aid your research?

☐ Engage with real estate professionals in the areas that you're interested in and begin researching comparable properties. This will give you a feel for the desirable property characteristics for the suburbs you are analysing, as well as the types of tenants you are likely to attract. Comparable sales will give you an understanding of the price ranges that properties are selling for and which characteristics are the most sought after.

☐ Attend property inspections and begin making your financial calculations. For all of the different properties you're interested in, practise calculating the rental yield, capital growth projections and budget expectations. What rental income do you think the property will be able to generate, and will this cover your mortgage repayments and other expenses? If not, plan how you will supplement your property's emergency fund when repairs and other expenses are eventually incurred.

☐ Once you've conducted your calculations, engage with a local property manager and request a rental appraisal. This property manager should be the same person who you plan to use to manage the property if/when you secure it. This way, the property manager will have confidence in their own rental appraisal.

☐ Once you've found a property that satisfies your due diligence calculations, engage with the listing agent and submit an offer. Ensure you stay in contact with the agent after you've begun negotiating. Sometimes negotiation periods can start and end quickly, and you don't want to miss out on the property because you forgot to answer your phone. Understand your personal budget and ensure you don't offer more than what you believe the property is worth.

☐ If your offer is accepted, congratulations! You've now entered the exchange period. At this stage, you will liaise with your solicitor, who will help manage the acquisition to ensure there are no problems. Your mortgage broker will also assist in preparing your loan and sourcing a property valuation from the lender.

☐ A building and pest inspection is an absolute must to ensure you're purchasing a quality property. This inspection can be completed before or after your offer is submitted.

☐ Once the conditions of the contract have been met and finances are ready to go, the property then settles. This signifies the formal transfer of the land title between the vendor and you as the buyer.

☐ After settlement, it's time for your property manager to begin advertising the property for potential tenants. If the vendor of the property agrees, sometimes early access to the property can be granted to the buyer so that the property manager can prepare the property for tenanting earlier.

☐ Once the property manager has successfully found a suitable tenant, the new tenant will move in and begin paying rental income. This will assist you as the buyer to pay for mortgage repayments and other expenses.

☐ After this step, you have achieved successful property investorship!

It's crucial to remember that these steps will vary due to many different circumstances, including the state or territory you buy in, whether the property was bought at auction or through negotiations, and other variables. But as a guide, these steps provide you with the foresight needed to conduct all of your market research and find some great professionals to join your trusted team.

Good luck for your next acquisition, and remember that preparation is key!

# ACKNOWLEDGEMENTS

We would like to offer our sincere gratitude to everyone who has supported us in writing this book.

First and foremost, we'd like to thank our friends and family – specifically Brian, Kylie and Rebecca. Your continuous support and encouragement was pivotal throughout our journey, and we can't thank you enough.

To Lesley and Eleanor from Major Street Publishing, thank you for believing in our vision and for enabling our book to come to life. Writing this book has been a dream of ours since the very beginning of our investing journey and we're elated to share our knowledge and experience with Australian investors, nationwide. Thank you for your encouragement, support and guidance.

To our incredible editor, Brooke, thank you for your support, enthusiasm and laughter. This book couldn't have come together without your expertise and keen eye for detail.

To all of our professional mentors in the industry, particularly Jeremy, thank you for sharing your sage knowledge and experience. We are sincerely grateful for the time and expertise you have imparted to us over the years.

# ABOUT THE AUTHORS

## LACHLAN VIDLER

Lachlan began his professional career as a Maritime Warfare Officer in the Royal Australian Navy. Throughout his naval career, Lachlan served on four ships and two military operations before finishing his time in the Navy as a Maritime Logistics Officer. After leaving the Navy, Lachlan went on to become a management consultant with Deloitte Australia and Accenture Australia. In these roles, Lachlan consulted to a wide range of clients and was responsible for implementing multimillion-dollar strategic projects within organisations.

Lachlan founded Atlas Property Group, an investment-focused residential buyer's agency, and currently serves as its director. In his role, Lachlan helps a wide range of investors purchase investment properties around Australia to further their own dreams of financial freedom.

Lachlan holds as Bachelor of Business and a Master of Commerce (Finance) from the University of New South Wales and a Graduate Certificate in Property Investment from Western Sydney University. Lachlan is currently completing a Master of Property Investment and Development at Western Sydney University.

Lachlan is a licensed real estate agent across multiple states and territories in Australia and is a member of the Property Investment Professionals of Australia.

In his personal life, Lachlan has built a multimillion-dollar property portfolio with his partner, Tori, and they have also undertaken property development activities. Lachlan thoroughly enjoys all manner of sports, travelling across the world and spending time with his friends and family.

## TORI COLLS

Tori began her professional career as an Intelligence Officer in the Royal Australian Air Force (RAAF). During her time in the RAAF, Tori has worked across numerous strategic and operational intelligence agencies, both within Australia and in the United States. This work contributed to a wide range of military operations and exercises, both at home and abroad.

Tori holds a Bachelor of Business and a Master of Project Management from the University of New South Wales and is currently undertaking a Master of Property Investment and Development at Western Sydney University.

Tori departed her full-time position in the RAAF to apply her business knowledge and experience as a management consultant with global consulting powerhouse Accenture Australia. Tori consults to a wide range of clients to resolve organisational issues and advance modernisation efforts.

After supporting Lachlan in his journey founding Atlas Property Group, Tori went on to assume the position of General Manager. In her role, Tori provides seamless business support to Atlas Property Group while also ensuring a first-class experience for all clients in their property investing journey.

Tori is a licensed real estate agent and also holds membership with the Australian Institute of Project Management and Property Investment Professionals of Australia.

Tori greatly enjoys interior architecture and design, taking time for travel, long-distance running and walking her and Lachlan's dog, Apollo.

## atlas
### PROPERTY
### GROUP

**ATLAS PROPERTY GROUP**

Atlas Property Group is an exclusive buyer's agency that helps a broad range of clients, each with their own unique goals and requirements, find high-quality investment-grade properties to complement and grow their portfolios.

The word 'Atlas' denotes a collection of maps that you can use to arrive at a destination. The Atlas Property Group logo embodies the notion of continuous personal development and a sense of 'journey', which is encapsulated by the 'steps' component of the branding.

**CONTACT US**

If you're a first-time buyer or seasoned investor looking to scale your existing portfolio, the team at Atlas Property Group is here to help you achieve your property goals!

Join our incredible team of clients who have successfully commenced their journey towards financial freedom through leveraging the power of property. Please visit www.atlaspropertygroup.com.au or call us on 1300 258 976 to learn more.

If you have any questions or feedback regarding *A Military Guide To Property Investing*, please forward them to book@atlaspropertygroup.com.au and the Atlas Property Group team will be in touch.

# REFERENCES

### Step 1: Reveille

Association of Superannuation Funds of Australia Limited 2018, *ASFA Retirement Standard*, superannuation.asn.au/ArticleDocuments/269/ASFA-RetirementStandard-Summary-2018.pdf.aspx?Embed=Y.

### Step 2: Discipline

Australian Securities Exchange 2020, *ASX Australian Investor Study 2020*, www2.asx.com.au/blog/australian-investor-study.

ANZ 2019, *Housing Affordability Report*, news.anz.com/content/dam/bluenotes/images/articles/2019/November/ANZ-Housing-Affordibility-report-Nov2019.pdf.

### Step 4: Professional mastery

Australian Government 2018, *Taxation Statistics 2017-18*, data.gov.au/data/dataset/taxation-statistics-2017-18.

Abelson, P & Chung, D 2004, *Housing prices in Australia: 1970 to 2003*, Macquarie University, econ.mq.edu.au/__data/assets/pdf_file/0018/220581/Abelson_9_04.pdf.

Razaghi, T 2021, 'Sydney house prices soar to record median of $1.3m after fastest quarterly rise in 28 years', Domain, domain.com.au/news/sydney-house-prices-soar-to-record-median-of-1309195-after-fastest-quarterly-rise-in-28-years-1048412.

### Step 5: Excellence

CoreLogic 2021, *Housing Market Update*, corelogic.com.au/reports/housing-market-update.

### Step 7: Courage

Australian Government 2018, *Taxation Statistics 2017-18*, data.
gov.au/data/dataset/taxation-statistics-2017-18.

Australian Securities Exchange 2020, *ASX Australian Investor
Study 2020*, www2.asx.com.au/blog/australian-investor-study.

Kohler, M & van der Merwe, M 2015, *Long-run Trends in Housing
Price Growth*, Reserve Bank of Australia, rba.gov.au/publications/
bulletin/2015/sep/3.html?fbclid=IwAR3CbBLgeKILST
HatSNrmBIho9U_hwzOLfKxNF7m0L1-JHKzwZIs0pw8mnc.

Clare, R 2019, *Better Retirement Outcomes: a snapshot of account
balances in Australia*, ASFA, www.superannuation.asn.au/
ArticleDocuments/359/1907-Better-Retirement-Outcomes-a-
snapshot-of-account-balances-in-Australia.pdf.aspx.

### Step 9: Dedication

Australian Government 2018, *Taxation Statistics 2017-18*, data.
gov.au/data/dataset/taxation-statistics-2017-18.

# INDEX

**major st** PUBLISHING

We hope you enjoy reading this book. We'd love you to post a review on social media or your favourite bookseller site. Please include the hashtag #majorstreetpublishing.

Major Street Publishing specialises in business, leadership, personal finance and motivational non-fiction books. If you'd like to receive regular updates about new Major Street books, email info@majorstreet.com.au and ask to be added to our mailing list.

Visit majorstreet.com.au to find out more about our books and authors.

We'd love you to follow us on social media.

- [in] linkedin.com/company/major-street-publishing
- [f] facebook.com/MajorStreetPublishing
- [○] instagram.com/majorstreetpublishing
- [y] @MajorStreetPub